Published by Periplus Editions (HK) Ltd.
with editorial offices at
5 Little Road #08-01
Singapore 536983

Copyright © 2000
Periplus Editions (HK) Ltd.

ISBN: 962-593-504-5

Library of Congress
Card Number: 00-107031

Publisher: Eric Oey
Associate Publisher: Christina Ong
Editor: Philip Tatham
Recipe Development: Benedetta Veronelli
Text Consultant: Marc Tibaldi
Translator: Natalie Danford
Coordinator: Sebastian Gutmann
Production: Violet Wong

Painting on endpapers by
Gianni Bertini

Photo Credits:
All food and location photography by Luca Invernizzi Tettoni. Additional photos by: The Image Bank Milan (Guido Alberto Rossi), pp. 4, 6; The Image Bank Milan (A. Lanzellotto), p. 21; Gran Caffè Ristorante Quadri, p. 23. Reproductions of paintings courtesy Galleria dell'Academia, Venice, Italy/Bridgeman Art Library, p. 12; and Ca' Rezzonico, Museo del Settecento, Venice, Italy/Bridgeman Art Library, p.13.

Distributors

North America
Tuttle Publishing
Distribution Center
Airport Industrial Park
364 Innovation Drive
North Clarendon, VT 05759-9436
Tel: (802) 773-8930
Fax: (802) 773-6993

Japan
Tuttle Publishing
RK Building 2nd Floor
2-13-10 Shimo Meguro, Meguro-Ku
Tokyo 153 0064
Tel: (81-3) 5437-0171
Fax: (81-3) 5437-0755

Asia Pacific
Berkeley Books Pte. Ltd.
5 Little Road #08-01
Singapore 536983
Tel: (65) 280-1330
Fax: (65) 280-6290

First Edition
1 3 5 7 9 10 8 6 4 2
05 04 03 02 01 00
PRINTED IN SINGAPORE

THE FOOD OF
VENICE

Authentic Recipes from the City of Romance

By Luigi Veronelli
Photography by Luca Invernizzi Tettoni
Styling by Christina Ong & Luca Invernizzi Tettoni

Featuring recipes from the following restaurants:

Antico Martini   Ai Gondolieri
Ca' Masieri   Ai Mercanti
La Caravella   Parco Gambrinus
Corte Sconta   Quadri
Al Covo   Alle Testiere
Fiaschetteria Toscana   Vini da Gigio
Da Fiore

PERIPLUS

Contents

Part One: Food in Venice

The richness of Venetian life is reflected in its cuisine

Rising majestically from the water, with an extensive network of canals as roads, Venice is a city like no other. This utopia, floating between the lagoon and sky, is much loved for its unique architecture—the ornate palazzi that line the Grand Canal, the forbidding Bridge of Sighs, and the ever-imposing Piazza San Marco—for its gondolas and gondoliers, its inviting *bàcari* or wine bars, and, of course, for its food.

The lagoon is the key to understanding the fundamentals of Venetian cuisine—for here the earth and sea become one. The lagoon plays host to innumerable species of the best and most flavorful fish in the Mediterranean; it is home to indigenous and migratory wild birds; and its many small islands provide ideal growing conditions for an array of unusual vegetables.

It is seafood, however, that has always been central to Venetian life. Not only was it an important part of the diet, it also served many other purposes. The penetrating smell of fish—or *freschino* as the Venetians call it—was once an omnipresent aroma since fish was used to feed farm animals and fish oil was used both as fuel and to preserve wood in the construction of boats and houses.

A large part of Venice's fortune stems from its pivotal position in the spice trade. The contributions made to Venetian cuisine by spices may not be immediately apparent, but they are instrumental in enriching the variety, flavors, and colors of Venetian food. Similarly, the foreign merchants and immigrant communities that sprung up in Venice all played their part in shaping the cuisine. The resultant cuisine was then popularized throughout Europe by travelling Venetians, especially the more conspicuous ones.

"My mother gave birth to me in Venice on April 2, Easter of the year 1725. She was craving shrimp. I like shrimp a lot." So begins the autobiography of one of Venice's most famous inhabitants, Giovanni Giacomo Casanova. Casanova was the son of actors who were part of the troupe of Carlo Goldoni, the city's most acclaimed playwright.

As an epicure, seducer, and traveler, Casanova was first and foremost a Venetian, and in his autobiography Casanova admits to preferring the food of his birthplace above all others. The pleasures of the table and of good company were for him the first steps towards eroticism and success—in this way, Casanova and Venice teach us about the love of pleasure, taste, and of sensitivity.

Cooking is the art of transforming nature's offerings through the culture, experience, and invention of a people, and Venetian cooking is no exception. It contains the grandeur of the city's history and reflects the richness of its art.

Page 2:
Sunset over Piazza San Marco (St. Mark's Square). The present shape of the piazza was created in the twelfth century for the meeting of Pope Alexander III and the Emperor Barbarossa.
Opposite:
Commanding stunning views across Piazza San Marco is Gran Caffè Ristorante Quadri, one of the grand dames of the Venetian dining scene. The restaurant has been in operation since 1775.

A Unique Lagoon Ecosystem

The water, air, and lagoon islands
provide an abundance of fish, fowl, and vegetable produce

The Venetian lagoon is a long, shimmering crescent of brackish water, separated from the Adriatic Sea by several narrow, fertile islands. Although recent archaeological evidence suggests that the lagoon may have been inhabited for two thousand years, the first major influx of people arrived in the fifth century, seeking refuge on the islands following Attila the Hun's invasion of Italy in AD 452. After the invader's withdrawal, many of the refugees returned home to the mainland. Some, however, elected to stay. The population of this nascent community was further augmented one hundred years later by a second wave of migrants: main-landers displaced by the Lombard invasion of northern Italy in AD 568.

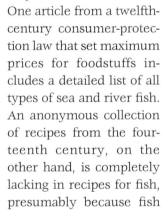

Out of necessity, the earliest Venetians—the lagoon inhabitants—became fishermen and boat-men and drew sustenance almost exclusively from the sea. They ate simply, relying on a diet of fresh fish cooked over an open flame. They also ate wild birds and game, and cultivated a wide variety of vegetables. Today, most of the islands are uninhabited but the lagoon still constitutes a unique ecosystem. It boasts certain species of fish and shellfish that are unique to the area; the same can be said of some wild birds that live in the lagoon, as well as the wild greens foraged on land.

Historical documents illustrate the key role played by fish in the history of the food of Venice. One article from a twelfth-century consumer-protection law that set maximum prices for foodstuffs includes a detailed list of all types of sea and river fish. An anonymous collection of recipes from the four-teenth century, on the other hand, is completely lacking in recipes for fish, presumably because fish were so common and familiar that no guidance was required for their preparation. Scholar Marino Sanudo, whose diaries and history of Venice are some of the best records of life at the turn of the sixteenth century, wrote that the Rialto and San Marco fish markets sold more than sixty different types of fish and seafood.

One particular fishing technique that was developed in the lagoon (and which was later

Opposite: Torcello was one of the earliest inhabited islands in the lagoon and once supported a thriving community of 20,000 before its decline in the fourteenth century. Today, all that remain are two pre twelfth-century churches and a very much reduced population.
***Left:** Venetians have relied on the Rialto market for fresh seafood since the beginning of the twelfth century.*

adopted as a pastime for noblemen) involved the use of a cormorant, a species of seabird that is a keen hunter of fish. A cormorant was caught and tied to the prow of a boat with a long cord. A ring was then placed around the bird's neck so that when it did catch a fish it would be unable to swallow it. As soon as the bird surfaced with a fish in its beak, the fishermen would pull on the cord to reel the bird in and then extract the fish from its mouth.

For both environmental and industrial reasons, there is now less commercial fishing in the Venetian lagoon than in the past, but local fishermen do still fish for many fish, eels, soft-shelled crabs, and other local specialties. The lagoon supports a wide variety of fish and shellfish, many of which are migrants rather than permanent residents.

Among the most prized fish from the lagoon are turbot, eel, gilthead, Saint Peter's fish (or John Dory), sole, and bass. Young bass are known as *baicolo* in the Venetian dialect and have lent their name to the *baicolo* cookie which is oval in shape and is thought to resemble the fish. The goby, or *gò* as it is known in Venice, is another lagoon resident that features prominently in local risottos and fish soups. Although it may be fried, it is usually boiled then strained to yield a thick liquid as in *risotto di gò e bevarasse* (goby and clam risotto).

The preparation of these myriad types of fish has remained simple over the centuries. In those days, as now, medium-sized fish were most often grilled. At one time fish were cooked on a spit, but today fish are cooked this way only on a few fishermen's islands, and even then, this type of preparation is reserved for specific types of fish, such as eel. Small fish were, and still are, fried. Grilled fish are generally served cold, whereas fried fish are served immediately while hot and crunchy. Certain types of fish are appropriate for boiling, mainly those that are large or especially fatty.

The Venetian diet also reflects the abundance of shellfish in the surrounding lagoon. No meal is complete without an antipasti of raw or lightly cooked shellfish. Among the more popular molluscs are clams and razor clams, scallops, mussels, and murex. Murex are slightly elongated spiny one-valve

of the lagoon. The hunter pursued the game using two crossed oars to propel the boat, and would then switch to a single, smaller paddle as he neared his prey. Finally, he would shoot the bird with a musket, called a *sciopo*, from which the boat got its name.

Today, snipes, mallards and other wild ducks, guinea fowl, partridges, and pheasants are first tenderized and then stuffed with sage, rosemary, and other herbs and roasted on a spit. Small game birds, such as thrushes, sparrows, and quail, are often threaded on skewers alternately with pieces of lean pork or slices of pancetta or lard, and served alongside polenta.

molluscs that are usually boiled then eaten cold. Other revered shellfish include octopus and baby octopus, cuttlefish, crabs, and shrimp. One particular specialty of the region is soft-shelled crab. This is, in fact, a normal crab that has recently molted and whose new shell has yet to harden. To prepare the famous *moleche con il pien* (stuffed soft-shelled crab), the live crabs are submerged for several hours in a mixture of beaten egg and cheese until they are dead and have literally stuffed themselves with the mixture. They are then dredged in flour, fried, and served as is, together with slices of grilled polenta.

Frequently, the same early inhabitants who worked as fishermen also hunted birds. These hunters first walked the shoals with nets and arrows, and later with muskets that were balanced on the prows of their boats. *Scioponi*—small low-lying boats—were ideal for navigating the marshy waters

The island soil, coupled with the warm and humid weather, and the lagoon's salty air, provide optimal growing conditions for certain types of produce. Artichokes (particularly the local *castraure*), asparagus, hops, and squash all flourish here. Other crops include peas, zucchini, string beans, peppers, fennel, and cabbage. All of these vegetables are prepared simply, often sautéed in olive oil with a clove of garlic and some herbs and spices.

Over the years, Venice has developed some rich and elaborate dishes that appear somewhat removed from the humble beginnings of Venetian cuisine. However, as a whole, the food of Venice remains simple and pure, and the legacy of those early lagoon inhabitants is plain to see in the many home-cooked and *trattoria* dishes.

Gateway to the East

*Like the architecture of the Basilica di San Marco,
Venetian food reflects the city's many foreign influences*

The Venetian Republic—which lasted from the election of its first doge, or chief magistrate, in AD 697, until Napoleon's invasion of the city and its subsequent handover to the Austrians in 1797—was always open to outsiders, who brought both money and business to the lagoon city and the surrounding towns. Venice hosted large groups of merchants and communities of foreigners—Armenians, Slavs, Greeks, Syrians, and others—who came both to buy and to sell goods. Venice was the gateway connecting the Far East to Europe, and transactions between these two parts of the world made the city even wealthier. The Far Eastern merchants—and all the other foreigners who came to reside in Venice, or who simply passed through—contributed to the shaping of the local palate.

The spice trade in particular was a Venetian specialty (as was slave trading early on, a legacy of which Venetians are less proud, but which nevertheless brought foreigners and foreign influence to their city). The first "spice route" ran across the Asian mainland, but by the turn of the fourteenth century that route had become unsafe. A new route was forged which ran from the East Indies all the way to Aleppo, Damascus, or Constantinople (Istanbul), and from there it was the Italians—Venetians and their archrivals, the Genovese—who shipped spices to Europe. Spice trading was dangerous and risky, but also highly profitable. One saying had it that a merchant who shipped six boatloads and lost five would still turn a profit on the remaining one. Another way to think of it was this: much of the Renaissance wealth of Venice, which lives on today in its art and architecture, was funded by the spice trade. Clove, nutmeg, cinnamon, and pepper were among the spices imported to add interest to European dishes, to preserve food, and for medicinal purposes.

Since they were so heavily involved in the spice trade, it was only natural that Venetians would incorporate spices into their cuisine. At the same time, many of the foreigners visiting and living in

Venice came from countries where spices were frequently used. The results of this evolutionary process are clear in many classic Venetian recipes. The cinnamon stick in *riso in cavroman* (rice with lamb), itself an imported dish from Dalmatia, and the pinch of saffron in *zuppa di pesce e verdure* (fish and vegetable soup) are both inherited from Venice's long legacy of spice trading. Such foreign influences were in evidence early. By the tenth century, local Venetian products were already being enlivened with additions from overseas colonies, including raisins, dates, and citrus fruits. As the ever-expanding empire came to include many of today's Italian cities, such as Brescia and Verona, as well as more distant places like Dalmatia and Constantinople, foreign influences would only grow.

Even today, spices that remain unknown in other Italian cities abound in Venice. For example, the recipe for *filetti di San Pietro in salsa d'arancia* (Saint Peter's fish in orange sauce) is a thoroughly modern creation from one of Venice's finest restaurants, but its use of ginger renders it unusual in Italy. The same can be said of the cloves in *crema di borlotti con porri e cozze* (bean soup with leeks and mussels) and the coriander seeds in *tonno marinato all'aceto*

This 18th-century painting by Pietro Longhi (school of), depicts a grand banquet held in the house of Nani in the Giudecca quarter.

balsamico (tuna marinated in balsamic vinegar).

Among the many contributions to Venetian cuisine, that of the Jews stands out. Jews first arrived in the Venice area in the twelfth century, when they settled in Mestre, on the mainland. In 1516, a segregated Jewish neighborhood was created in Venice itself. The Jewish community grew quite large and varied, drawing Jews from Austria to the north, from Spain and the south of Italy, and from even farther away. It eventually supported five synagogues, each one serving a different segment of the community. Today there are about six hundred Jews remaining in Venice.

Jews, who had lived in foreign countries since the time of the Diaspora, had already developed a tradition of adapting the food of their adopted communities to meet *kashruth*, or kosher, laws. This meant that in Venice, Jews could eat fish but not shellfish. They substituted pork products with duck, turkey, and goose, which had a similarly rich flavor. The pairing of rice with various types of vegetables, particularly artichokes, also evolved from within the Jewish community.

Numerous modifications to the Basilica di San Marco have resulted in a building that exhibits a mixture of different styles and influences.

When Napoleon took over Venice in 1797, he not only allowed Jews to leave their neighborhood, but also brought further change to the city by handing it over to the Austrians under the Treaty of Campo Formio. The nineteenth-century Austrian Empire brought numerous new culinary influences to Venice. Its contributions to Venetian cuisine include the chiffel (a type of almond croissant,) and the so-called spritz (nothing more than a mixture of wine and water that was developed further in Venice with the addition of bitters or liqueurs).

Although fiercely proud of their culinary tradition, Venetians in earlier times were not shy about adopting new foods, so while corn was indigenous to the Americas—and introduced to Europe by a returning Christopher Columbus in 1493—polenta has sustained Venetians for centuries.

Sometimes it seems that none of Venice's typical foods are indigenous. Even the city's famous *bac-cala* and *stoccafisso*, two forms of dried cod, considered by many to be the ur-foods of Venice, can be claimed by another culture. In January 1432, Venetian nobleman Pietro Querini was shipwrecked near the Lofoten Islands in northern Norway. Thanks to this accident, Querini came to know the residents of those islands and learned about fishing for cod as well as methods for drying and then rehydrating the dried fish. Querini brought these dried products—salt-preserved *baccalà* and air-dried stockfish—back to Venice with him, and his fellow Venetians soon became enamored of them. The use of dried fish spread quickly from the coastal city to the towns and villages farther inland, where fresh fish was difficult to obtain.

Naturally, sailors were quick to adopt this new item, which could be stored almost indefinitely and allowed them to stay at sea for long periods of time. The simple flavors of the fish were subsequently enlivened by the addition of herbs, and the dish was elevated from the tables of farmers and seamen to those of noblemen. The need to preserve food also gave birth to one of the city's oldest recipes and one of its most symbolic: fish in *saor* sauce, a savory preparation containing onion, vinegar, pine nuts, and raisins, which stayed fresh for at least one week, if not longer.

Not only was Venice a magnet for travelers and traders, it spawned travelers and traders of its own, the most famous of whom was Marco Polo. Even if Marco Polo was not responsible for the introduction of pasta to Italy, as popular legend would have it, Venice did enjoy a cuisine imbued with many exotic foreign influences.

Salt, Sugar, and Rice

How salt, sugar, and rice influenced the history of Venice

Three of the world's most basic foodstuffs—salt, rice, and sugar—not only play an important role in Venetian cooking, but have shaped its history as well. In modern times, we rarely give salt much thought; it is everywhere and therefore invisible. But salt is a key ingredient in every cuisine on earth, and its history intersects with that of the Venetian Republic, which lasted from the mid-twelfth century until 1797. Back in the eighth century, when the first Venetians established homes on the islands in the lagoon, the only resource they had close at hand was the sea, and as a result salt and fish were the only items they could produce and eat. They bartered these with others living on the mainland in order to obtain meat, wheat, and cloth.

As Venice grew in wealth, so did the elaborateness of its famed carnival.

Eventually, these early Venetians grew wealthier and increased both their trade and their fleets of ships. By AD 932, the Venetians had only one rival in the salt trade, the town of Comacchio. They put an end to that rivalry by attacking Comacchio, and they then enjoyed a monopoly on salt, both that of their own making from the salt pans of nearby Chioggia as well as salt imported from other areas. The old Salt Office, a warehouse built to contain 44,000 tons of salt, is still in existence in Venice today, where a portion of it is used as a boatyard.

Salt was crucial not just for seasoning food, but for preserving food. Salt preservation made it possible to keep seasonal items available year-round; it also meant that Venetian travelers could stock up on preserved products before embarking on long journeys. Such products both sustained them during travel and served as their stock-in-trade. Back home, Venetian markets have long offered all types of prosciutto, sausages, salami, and other cold cuts, all made with salt. The market stalls also offer *salami de mar* (seafood salami), made with sturgeon and tuna and formed through salting (it may also be air-dried, smoked, or pickled). In the days before refrigeration, Venetians kept oysters fresh by keeping them in barrels full of seawater. Oysters stored this way not only stayed edible, they could also be exported as far as Vienna and Budapest without going bad.

One of the most important products to be shipped "in salt" was the body of Saint Mark, the patron saint of Venice. In AD 828, a group of Venetians stole the body of their city's patron saint right out of its coffin in Alexandria and hid it in a large cargo of salt. (Obtaining the corpses of saints was one way that nascent city-states established themselves in those days. As of the year 1519, Venetian patriots were responsible for absconding with fifty-five different saints' bodies, as well as various body parts). They then transported the body of Saint Mark back to Venice without incident. Legend has it that a blustery storm, presumably conjured up by the saint himself, blew them directly to their destination.

Venetians ruled not only the salt trade, but the spice trade as well, which in those days included trafficking in sugar. Sugar and spices were key to establishing the city as one of three central trade points early in the eleventh century, when *sacchetis Venetis* (bags of assorted spices) were already being sold by the city's traders. Initially, sugar was sold via pharmacies at a high price, and it was subdivided into several different categories, including the expensive *mucchera*, which Venetians claimed had been twice refined and which was said to be produced in Egypt for the Sultan of Babylon. As early as AD 966, a large warehouse was constructed for sugar that was imported from the East, then exported to Central Europe. The Cornaro family, who controlled much of the sugar trade in and out of Venice, was wealth-

The canals of Venice were once busy with barges and other boats transporting goods from the ships to the warehouses, and are lined with the grand houses of wealthy traders.

ier than most royalty at the time.

Venetians were not content merely to trade in sugar, however, and eventually they opened the first true industrial sugar refinery, modeled on factories they had seen in Turkey. With the high yield from the refinery, and the high prices they continued to charge, Venetians prospered, until Spanish and Portuguese colonists created competing refineries in the West Indies and elsewhere. Sugar was a sweetener, but it was also used for more artistic purposes. Wealthy Venetians reveled in elaborate confectionery creations. When Duchess Beatrice d'Este of Milan visited Venice in 1493, she was served a meal of 300 different items, all made of sugar. In 1574, an even more ostentatious spread was prepared for Henry III of France: he arrived at a banquet to find that all 1,286 items on the table, including bread, silverware, tablecloth, napkins, and centerpiece, had been sculpted of spun sugar. Venetians today are unlikely to prepare such sugar sculptures, but they still enjoy a taste for sweets such as cookies, *favette* (fried sweets made with grappa), donuts, candied and caramelized fruit, and sugar-coated almonds.

Rice is unlikely to serve as a medium for any new art forms, but it is still difficult to imagine a time when it was not easily available in Venice, since so few meals there begin without rice in some form. In Venice, *primi*, as Italians call their first courses, are less likely to consist of pasta and more likely to feature rice, which is served both in soup and in the form of risotto and other dishes. There is scarcely a vegetable available that the people of Venice have failed to combine with rice. They serve rice with beans, cabbage, potatoes, leeks, asparagus, and squash, just to name a few. Rice was not indigenous

to the area, however. It was introduced to Venice during the Middle Ages by travelers from the Far East (and it is one of the many products that Venetian explorer Marco Polo may or may not have brought back from the Orient). Although it caught on quickly, like sugar, it was initially considered more medicinal than nutritious. Pharmacies sold rice at high prices, and it was counted out grain by grain. Most of this rice was ground in a mortar into a soft, fine flour and then used to thicken soup.

It was during the sixteenth century that rice became fundamental to the diet of Venetians, more for economic reasons than for reasons of taste. It was during that century that the ducal government decided to provide incentives for the production of rice in the Po Valley by making the cultivation of rice a tax-free enterprise. Naturally, farmers were happy to grow it in large amounts, and a network of deep troughs was dug in the countryside of the Veneto in order to create the damp environment needed to grow rice. The habit of eating rice has stuck with Venetians, and today, *Risi e Bisi* (Rice with Peas), a delicious dish that falls somewhere between a soup and a risotto, is the city's most famous dish and is consumed on St. Mark's day, a holiday commemorating Venice's patron saint.

Whetting Your Appetite

In Venice, gluttony is raised to an art form

Venetians eat two meals a day, just as all Italians do. They eat Italian-style, meaning that they rarely consume breakfast, but enjoy a light lunch, and a complete dinner. And, as in most parts of Italy, a full meal in Venice follows very specific steps: *antipasto* (appetizer), *primo* (first course), *secondo* (main course) accompanied by one or more *contorni* (side dishes), and *dolce* (dessert). However, whereas most *antipasti* consist of salami, in Venice they comprise almost exclusively fish and shellfish. In the rest of Italy, classic first courses are pasta dishes in some form or another, but Venetians are more likely to sit down to a risotto or soup. And Venice's most favored main courses, in addition to relying on fish, characteristically make use of organ meats, wild duck, and other game. But the biggest difference between general Italian and Venetian eating habits lies in frequency. While most Italians seem satisfied with those two full meals a day, and perhaps an afternoon nibble, Venetians give the impression of snacking all day long.

First, there are the cafés. Venice can be credited with introducing coffee to the western world—coffee in the form of a drink arrived in Venice in 1640 by way of Turkey. By the time Venetian playwright Carlo Goldoni wrote one of his most famous plays, *La Bottega del Caffè* (*The Coffeehouse*), in the eighteenth century, establishments specializing in coffee were already familiar to his audiences. The play illustrates the role of coffee houses at that time: they were houses of ill repute, frequented by gamblers, con artists, and men and women of loose morals, although nobles were not above paying visits to them. Coffeehouses were open until the wee hours of the morning, if not twenty-four hours a day. As time passed, coffeehouses became more acceptable to Venetian high society. By the close of the eighteenth century, there would be twenty-seven such coffeehouses in Venice's main piazza, St. Mark's Square.

In 1720, Floriano Francesconi opened Venezia Trionfante, or Triumphant Venice. Over the years, patrons affectionately referred to the café as

Opposite:
Good food is not restricted to grand restaurants. Alle Testiere is a small trattoria that, despite its size, is quintessentially Venetian. Pictured here are (in the foreground) ravioli alla zucca con salsa di scampi (pumpkin ravioli with shrimp sauce), and gnocchetti ai calamaretti (gnocchetti with baby calamari).

Left:
Caffè Florian is the oldest cafe in Venice—it first opened its doors on December 29 1720. Since then, it has served drinks to the likes of Byron, Dickens, Proust, Stravinsky, and, of course, Casanova.

Florian's, and "Caffè Florian" soon became Venice's most famous coffeehouse. Since opening, it has served as a vantage point from which the famous (including Byron, Goethe, and Dumas) and the unknown have observed the never-ending movement in the piazza. Caffè Florian was also a favorite hunting ground of Casanova since it was then the only café to admit women. Today, patrons sit outside during summer and listen to the music played by orchestras on the square. In winter, they retire to its cozy interior, which is decorated with paintings of famous Venetians.

Another quintessential Venetian landmark is Gran Caffè Ristorante Quadri, also located on St. Mark's Square. Quadri was opened in 1775, shortly before the Austrian occupation of Venice. After a difficult start, the café was finally endorsed by the nobility in the 1830s and has enjoyed a reputation for serving quality food and drink ever since.

While cafés have evolved over the years from disreputable places into refined spots, *bàcari* (wine bars) have maintained their proletarian atmosphere. Venetians make the rounds of *bàcari* for *ombre*—which literally means "shadows," but in this case refers to glasses of wine—before lunch and dinner. The etymology of the word *ombre* for glasses of wine is uncertain. Legend has it that long ago street vendors who sold wine in St. Mark's Square followed the shadow of the clock tower so that their wine would stay cool.

The word *bàcari* comes from the Venetian expression *bàcara* meaning "to have a good time," and, more specifically, to eat and drink with friends, which is precisely what goes on in these places.

Opposite and right: Whether dining inside or out, Gran Caffè Ristorante Quadri on Piazza San Marco is a feast for all the senses. Pictured opposite is a dessert of Gelato al Forno (Baked Ice Cream).

Today, such bars serve local wines from the Veneto and the nearby Friuli region, and they still specialize in *cicheti*, or Venetian snack foods. Most of these are fish-based, and they include such items as small savory tarts filled with puréed *baccalà*, sardines in *saor* or sweet-and-sour sauce, eggs with anchovies, and fritters. There are other snacks available as well: *cotechino* sausage on polenta, nerves, and the delicate *castraure* artichokes of Sant'Erasmo island. If you find yourself in one of Venice's *bàcari*, simply order a glass of wine and point to whatever looks good to eat. In *bàcari*, language matters little, conviviality is everything.

Naturally, Venice also boasts a large number of restaurants, many of them justifiably famous for their fresh fish, such as Al Covo and Trattoria Corte Sconta, and for their renditions of local favorites: Ai Mercanti offers tripe with rock salt, and Antico Martini a fabulous shrimp and arugula risotto.

In its heyday, the Venetian republic's influence extended far and wide and some of the cities that fell under its sphere of control are, today, part of the Veneto region, of which Venice is the capital. It is not surprising, therefore, that the traditions of some of these cities, particularly their architectural and culinary traditions, are closely linked to those of Venice. Most of these towns have their own special products (whether it be a vegetable, a fruit, a cheese, a type of fish, or a baked item), many of which have been absorbed into Venetian cuisine.

At one time Venice turned to nearby Chioggia— the town at the southernmost point of the lagoon— for its salt pans, and these supplied much of the salt that the city exported. Now Chioggia's most famous export is its yellow squash, known locally as "Chioggia veal" due to its tender consistency. Chioggia is one of Italy's busiest fishing ports which houses an international fish exchange. It is also famous for its fish stew, which combines a variety of fish and shell-fish, as well as a risotto featuring goby fish.

While Chioggia is celebrated for its squash, Treviso's claim to fame is radicchio, and it is completely justified, for Treviso radicchio—or *radicio Trevisan*, as it is known in Venetian—with its long, pointy leaves and meaty cores, provides the gold standard by which to judge all radicchio. It is at its finest when grilled simply at Treviso's own Gambrinus di San Polo di Piave. Much of Treviso's cuisine is similar to that of Venice—it uses plenty of fish and organ meats. Treviso is also rumored to have been the birthplace of tiramisù, a dessert of mascarpone cheese and ladyfingers which is now served throughout the world, but which naturally tastes best at its source.

In the center of the Veneto lies the charming city of Vicenza, famous for its wealth of Palladian architecture. Vicenza is known for its preparation of *baccalà*, which is served with polenta in a similar style as it is in Venice. Any self-respecting citizen, however, will haughtily inform you that the differences between *Baccalà alla Vicentina* and *Baccalà alla Veneziana* are myriad.

Don't be surprised if you spot some of these regional specialties on Venetian menus, and vice versa. While Italians are typically fiercely proud of the cuisines of their native cities, they are too full of culinary curiosity to ignore the foods of their close neighbors.

Part Two: The Venetian Kitchen

*Good quality, fresh basic ingredients
are all that is required to prepare delicious Venetian cuisine*

Venetian cooking relies on an array of standard cooking methods, such as grilling, sautéing, boiling, and roasting. Like most Italian cuisine, the food of Venice does not require many complicated techniques and is straightforward, relying instead on the natural flavors of fresh produce. And, since the equipment used does not differ from that which is found in any modern kitchen, cooking Venetian presents few problems to the home cook.

The most important items in the Venetian pantry are the same as those for any Italian cuisine: a good olive oil, grana cheese, and a suitable rice for making risotto. Apart from frying fish, when a light vegetable oil is often preferred, good quality extra virgin olive oil is essential for drizzling over *antipasti* or for use in cooked dishes.

Quality Parmigiano-Reggiano cheese is a must; packaged grated "parmesan" is convenient but is not a viable substitute for serious cooks. Avoid buying large quantities of the cheese as it may dry out.

When cooking risotto, an Italian rice such as arborio, carnaroli, or vialone nano is required.

Most important of all, however, is access to fresh vegetables and fish. The food of Venice is not difficult to master as long as you use good quality, fresh and flavorful basic ingredients.

Making Polenta

Traditionally, polenta is prepared in a large copper pot known as a *paiolo*, but any type of large pan will suffice. Although the cooking time here may seem excessive, don't try and skimp on it. You will end up with undercooked polenta that is bitter and hard to digest.

Rock salt to taste
6 cups (1½ liters) water
1 lb (500 g) cornmeal for polenta

In a large pot, bring generously salted water to a boil. As soon as it begins to boil, add the cornmeal very slowly in a thin stream, stirring continuoulsy with a wooden spoon. Continue stirring constantly, and in the same direction, until the polenta is extremely thick (stirring should be difficult) and can be pulled away from the sides of the pan, about 45 to 60 minutes. Serve the polenta warm, or pour onto a wooden board to cool. Cooled polenta may be cut into slices, which can then be toasted, fried, or grilled.

Opposite:
For a soft and creamy polenta, look for finely ground cornmeal, for a more unrefined, chewy polenta, use coarsley ground cornmeal.

Venetian Ingredients

*A list of common and unusual products
found in every well-stocked Venetian pantry*

Artichokes

Arugula

Baccalà

ARTICHOKE: There are two types of artichoke eaten in Venice, the regular variety, known as *articioco* in Venetian, and the baby variety known as *castraura* or *carciofino*. The common *articiochi* are prepared and eaten in the usual way: after being steamed or boiled, the outer leaves are plucked for the "meat" they contain at their axil. The fuzzy choke is often not as profuse as in other varieties but the tender heart is just as sweet. When preparing artichoke hearts, leave them in a bowl of cold water with a few drops of lemon juice added to prevent discoloration. *Castraure* are harvested when still small and young. The young shoots are pruned, leaving only a few artichoke to grow. *Castraure* are prized as a delicacy, the majority of it coming from Sant'Erasmo.

ARUGULA: The flavor and texture of this tasty green, also known as rocket, changes drastically over its lifespan. Young arugula leaves are soft and mild; more mature leaves are tougher and sharper, to the point of being peppery. When using arugula in salad, look for young, bright green leaves.

BACCALÀ: Venetians use the term baccalà to refer to stockfish, or cod that is air-dried to a rock-hard texture (in the rest of Italy, stockfish is called *stoccafisso*; and baccalà refers to salt-cod, or cod that is salted then partially dried). The moisture content of stockfish is reduced to around 15 percent which accounts for its stiffness and enables it to keep well. To rehydrate stockfish, the cod must be soaked in several changes of water for one to two days before being pounded while simultaneously adding a thin stream of olive oil. The result is a soft, white creamy mixture.

BAÌCOLI COOKIES: These simple, dry Venetian cookies are traditionally served alongside zabaione or with a sweet dessert wine for dunking. Substitute with cat's tongues or ladyfingers.

BORLOTTI BEANS: These small beans, which are sometimes labeled cranberry beans or Roman beans, are pink and beige and usually available in dried form. They are similar in flavor to kidney beans.

CALF'S LIVER: When purchasing liver, look for a shiny surface. Use any liver you do buy within twenty-four hours, as it doesn't keep well. If your butcher hasn't removed the membrane on the outer surface of the liver, do so before cooking.

CALF'S LUNG: Lung needs to be cooked at length in order to be edible. Ask your butcher to supply the lung already chopped.

CANESTRELLI: A type of scallop that is found only in Venice. Canestrelli are small and tender. As a substitute, purchase small sea scallops still in their shells.

CANNELLINI BEANS: These large white beans have a subtle flavor and soft texture. They are widely available in dried form.

CARLETTI: Wild greens are widely used in Italy. Carletti are similar in shape to dandelions and may be substituted with bitter greens, such as arugula, or a mix of bitter and mild greens, such as spinach. Wherever you live, there are sure to be local wild greens that would make a good substitute, but be sure to consult with an expert forager before eating anything.

CUTTLEFISH: These cephalopods are similar to squid and octopus. They contain a sac of black ink, which is usually used to flavor the dishes in which they are incorporated. The ink turns rice and pasta a dramatic black. Cuttlefish ink tagliatelli is packaged dried pasta made using cuttlefish ink.

GARDEN CRESS: Garden cress (*Lepidium sativum*) is sometimes known as pepper cress because of its spicy taste. Watercress is a member of the same family and makes a good substitute.

GILTHEAD FISH: This member of the *Sparus auratus* family is a type of sea bream commonly found in the Mediterranean. As the name implies, it has a very shiny head. Substitute any type of fleshy white fish for gilthead fish. Some good choices include sea bass and dorade.

GOBY FISH: This spiny fish (*Gobiidae*) lives in shallow, muddy water and is sometimes known as a mudsucker. If you cannot find goby fish, use any type of flat fish, such as skate, in its place.

GRANA CHEESE: Grana cheese is a large category of hard, dry cheeses that includes Parmesan cheese and Grana Padano cheese. These types of cheese are usually grated and sprinkled over pasta just before serving, or brought to the table so that each diner can serve him- or herself. Purchase chunks of such cheeses and grate them yourself, just before using. Pre-grated cheese dries out and loses much of its flavor.

GRAPPA: A dry, transparent, high-percentage alcohol made by distilling grape skins and vines that is usually consumed in small amounts after a meal. It is also used as an ingredient in some dishes. Grappa is available in most liquor stores.

MARJORAM: This herb, which is somewhat similar to fresh oregano, seems to brighten up just about any dish. Marjoram has tiny leaves, which should be removed from its tougher stems. Do not substitute dried marjoram for fresh.

MARSALA: This dark, sweet wine is almost syrupy in consistency. It adds depth to all kinds of desserts and some savory dishes as well.

MINT: Fresh mint leaves are a vivacious addition to many dishes. Leaves should be green with no yellowing around the edges. Remove the leaves from the stems before using.

MULLET: These fish, from the *Mugilidae* and *Mullidae* families are available in numerous forms. Look for red mullet, gray mullet, striped mullet, and white mullet. All are flavorful white fish with rich, tender flesh.

Borlotti (left) and cannellini beans

Carletti

Marjoram

Mint

Flat-leafed parsley

Porcini

Treviso radicchio

Rosemary

MUREX: This shellfish resides in a thick, rough, and sometimes spiny shell. If you cannot find murex, substitute with an equal amount of mussel meat or squid.

PANCETTA: Pancetta is often compared to American bacon, although it is not smoked. Pancetta is rolled up into a cylinder and then cured. It is sold in slices—usually thinner than slices of prosciutto or salami. Some recipes simply will not taste the same without the savory addition of a little pancetta, so make an effort to find the real thing at Italian specialty stores.

PARSLEY: Flat-leafed parsley—the variety used in Venice—is the most popular herb in European cookery. The stems and leaves are chopped up to use as a flavoring or as a garnish. Curly-leafed parsley possesses a slightly different flavor and is more commonly used as a garnish only.

POLENTA: Ground cornmeal is cooked into mush, then eaten either warm and soft or cooled and cut into slices (that may then be grilled). Look for imported Italian polenta in specialty stores. Steer clear of instant polenta.

PORCINI MUSHROOMS: Fresh porcini mushrooms are thick and meaty and have a strong aroma. Do not confuse them with dried porcini mushrooms, which are flavorful once rehydrated but cannot be used in salads as the fresh mushrooms can.

PROSECCO: This *spumante*, or sparkling wine, is the most frequently consumed in Italy. In Venice, the eternal Harry's Bar uses prosecco to make its famous Bellini, a peach-flavored concoction. Prosecco on its own stands as a perfect aperitif, though it may also be served with fish, cheese, and white meat.

RADICCHIO: Radicchio is a type of chicory lettuce. There are many different types of radicchio—all of which are red in color—but the one most prized in the Veneto is Treviso radicchio, which comes from the city of Treviso. This radicchio has long, pointy leaves that stand away from its central core. Like all chicory, radicchio is somewhat bitter, but its flavor softens and sweetens when it is cooked.

RISOTTO RICE: Risotto is a creamy rice dish made with certain kinds of Italian rice. The most common types of risotto rice are arborio rice, carnaroli rice, and vialone nano rice. All have short, stubby grains and cook to a satisfying, firm consistency.

ROSEMARY: A shrub native to the Mediterranean area, rosemary leaves are highly aromatic and are commonly used in Venice to flavor marinades, meat, and poultry dishes.

SAINT PETER'S FISH: Also known as John Dory, the white flesh of Saint Peter's fish is delicate and flavorful. So named because of the "thumbprints of Saint Peter" which are visible on either side of its body.

SALT-PRESERVED FISH: Venetians have a long history of preserving fish in salt, which kept it fresh long before refrigeration was invented. This method is today most commonly used with small fish. Italian specialty markets carry salt-preserved anchovies (far superior to those canned in oil), salt-preserved herring, and salt-preserved sardines. These need to be rinsed (or soaked in milk) to remove the salt. They also need to be boned, which is simply a matter of slitting their bellies and splitting each fish into two fillets. The bones should lift right out.

SAVOY CABBAGE: The cabbage most often used in Venice is Savoy cabbage, a variety with curly leaves and a slightly more delicate flavor than common green cabbage, which is also acceptable. Look for firm, tight heads. Avoid any yellow-looking cabbage. Fresh cabbage smells sweet and mild; the sulfurous odor many people associate with cabbage indicates that it is no longer fresh.

SCALLION: Also known as spring onions, scallions (used as a garnish or flavor enhancer) are sometimes treated as a vegetable in their own right and served as an appetizer or as a side dish.

SCAMPI: Known as Norway lobsters or Dublin Bay prawns in North America, and *langoustine* in France, these large shellfish—similar in size to small lobsters—are prized for their flesh which is more delicate than lobster. Substitute with jumbo shrimp.

SCORPION FISH: This is a flavorful, spiny fish considered so unattractive that to call someone a scorpion fish in Italy is to say that he or she is extremely ugly. As if to compensate for its unattractiveness, its meat is delicious. If you cannot find scorpion fish, red snapper makes a decent substitute.

SOFT-SHELLED CRAB: These crabs are not a different species from regular crabs, but simply crabs that have molted and have newly grown shells that are still soft and delicate. Purchase soft-shelled crabs live.

SOPPRESSATA: This pork salami is a Venetian specialty and can sometimes be found in Italian specialty stores. It consists of 65% lean pork and 35 percent pork fat.

SPLEEN: Like all organ meats, spleen should be cooked within twenty-four hours of purchase.

THYME: This herb works particularly well with all kinds of Mediterranean flavors. Fresh thyme leaves are green, but sometimes have a gray tint to them. A single sprig of thyme will have many small leaves. Sprigs of thyme are often used whole (sometimes as part of a bouquet garni), then removed before serving.

TRIPE: There are two kinds of tripe (which is part of a cow's stomach): smooth tripe, which has a smooth surface, and honeycomb tripe, which has a waffled appearance. Honeycomb tripe is generally more flavorful and tender. In Italy, tripe is soaked in lime, brined, and then boiled before it reaches the shelves, which reduces the cooking time considerably. If you purchase tripe that has not been prepared in advance, it will have to be boiled before being used in the following recipes.

VALERIANELLA LETTUCE: A mild lettuce in the Valerianella family, which includes corn salad, mâche, and lamb's lettuce. The leaves are so tender and soft that it is used exclusively for salad.

ZUCCHINI: These green vegetables are at their best in the spring. Look for firm-fleshed zucchini (courgettes) that haven't been punctured. Female zucchini are sometimes sold with their yellow flowers still attached. These are completely edible and make a lovely garnish.

Savoy cabbage

Thyme

Valerianella lettuce

Zucchini

Part Three: The Recipes

Antipasti, or appetizers, are traditionally served before the main meal proper but may also be taken as a light meal in themselves

Antipasto di Pesce
Fish Antipasto (Corte Sconta)

This antipasto spread actually consists of five separate simple dishes, all of which depend on your finding the freshest seafood available. Amounts can be varied to serve a crowd or a smaller group. Serve all five components together for an impressive opening to a Venetian meal, or as a light lunch.

Cicale di Mare (Mantis Shrimp)
Salt to taste
Mantis shrimp
½ cup (125 ml) white wine vinegar

Gamberetti (Small Shrimp)
Salt to taste
Live shrimp

Uova di Seppia
1 onion
1 carrot
1 stalk celery
Green peppercorns
Salt to taste
Cuttlefish eggs

Garusoli (Murex)
Salt to taste
Murex, cleaned in 7 changes of water

Measurements

Measurements in this book are given in volume as far as possible: 1 measuring **cup** contains 250 ml (roughly 8 oz); 1 **teaspoon** contains 5 ml, while 1 **tablespoon** contains 15 ml or the equivalent of 3 teaspoons. Australian readers please note that the standard Australian measuring spoon is larger, containing 20 ml or 4 teaspoons, so use only ¾ tablespoon when following the recipes. Where imperial measurements are given, approximate metric conversions follow in brackets.

Recipe titles

Names of dishes are given in Italian and in English. For those dishes that are commonly known by their Venetian names—in the local Venetian dialect—the Venetian title is given (inside quotation marks).

All restaurants are located in Venice unless otherwise stated.

Opposite:
From left: mantis shrimp, small shrimp, cuttlefish eggs, murex, and baby octopus.

Polpetti (Baby Octopus)
Salt to taste
Baby octopus, max 3 oz (90 g) each
1 cup (250 ml) white wine vinegar

For the **mantis shrimp**, bring a large pot of salted water to a boil. Add the crayfish. Return water to a boil and add vinegar. Remove from heat and remove crayfish immediately. Use kitchen scissors to cut along both sides of the tail. Carefully pull apart the shell and extract the meat.

For the **shrimp**, heat an iron lathe over an open flame. Also, bring a large pot of salted water to a boil. Add the live shrimp to the pot. When the shrimp float to the surface, remove from heat and submerge the extremely hot iron lathe into the water. (This will make it easier to shell the shrimp later.) After a few minutes, drain shrimp and shell carefully.

For the **cuttlefish eggs**, prepare a court-bouillon: in a large pot combine the onion, carrot, celery, and peppercorns. Add 4 cups (1 liter) of lightly salted water. Bring to a boil. Lower the heat and simmer for 30 minutes. Add the cuttlefish eggs to the court-bouillon and simmer them over medium heat for 15 minutes. Drain cuttlefish eggs and cut into strips.

For the **murex**, bring a large pot of salted water to a boil. Add the murex and cook, simmering briskly for $1\frac{1}{2}$ hours. Remove from the heat, but keep the murex in the boiling water. As soon as the murex are cool enough to touch, but still warm, remove them from the cooking water one at a time and, using a small metal pin, extract the meat. If part of the meat remains in the shell, crush the shell lightly and use the pin to remove it.

For the **baby octopus**, bring a large pot of salted water to a boil. Touch an octopus to the boiling water 2 or 3 times until its tentacles curl up, then add to the pot. Repeat with remaining octopus. Stir and add vinegar. Cook over medium heat, simmering, until tentacles are tender and can be pierced easily with a knife, about 20 minutes. Cut out eyes and mouth before serving.

Tonno Marinato all'Aceto Balsamico
Tuna Marinated in Balsamic Vinegar (Corte Sconta)
See the photograph on page 47.

Extra-virgin olive oil for dish and vinaigrette
1 1-lb (500-g) piece sushi-grade tuna, sliced
   into thin strips
3 teaspoons balsamic vinegar
Salt to taste
Pinch coriander seeds, ground
2 juniper berries, minced
10 oz (300 g) celery, cut into long strips

Lightly oil a casserole. In the casserole, arrange the tuna strips, leaving space in between them.

In a bowl, mix the vinegar with a small amount of salt. While whisking, add as much oil as necessary to create an emulsion. Add the coriander seeds and juniper berries and pour the vinaigrette over the tuna. Marinate for approximately 1 hour.

Just before serving, garnish the tuna with celery. Serve immediately. Serves 6.

Granceole alla Ricca • *Simmered Spider Crab*

Here spider crabs are gently simmered to bring out their delicate flavor. These call for a dry, elegant, young white wine, preferably a Breganze Bianco.

5 tablespoons butter
2 carrots, sliced
2 onions, sliced
6 cups (1½ liters) dry white wine
1 bouquet garni of bay leaf and flat-leaf parsley
2–3 black peppercorns
6 medium spider crabs, cleaned and rinsed
　　several times in cold water
Salt to taste
Juice of ½ lemon
Extra-virgin olive oil for dressing
Freshly ground black pepper to taste

To prepare the court-bouillon, melt the butter in a large pot over low heat. Add the carrots and onion and cook , but do not allow the onion to brown. Add the wine and 4 cups cold water, then add the bouquet garni and the peppercorns. Salt to taste.

Bring this mixture to a boil. Add the crabs, return to a boil, turns down to a simmer, and cook for 30 minutes. Remove the crabs from the liquid with a slotted spoon and allow to cool. Open the rear of the crabs where the shell is attached and scoop out the meat with a spoon. Dice the crabmeat and reserve. Thoroughly wash the shells, which should be bright red in color. To prepare the lemon sauce, in a small bowl dissolve a pinch of salt in the lemon juice. Add olive oil to taste. Whisk well, then add pepper to taste. Dress the diced crabmeat with this lemon sauce. Divide the crabmeat evenly among the 6 cleaned crab shells. Place the filled shells on 6 serving plates and serve immediately. Serves 6.

Cape Longhe in Padella • *Sautéed Razor Clams*

This recipe can also be made with mussels or with a combination of equal parts razor clams, cherry-stone clams, cockles, and mussels. Make sure to have additional crusty bread on hand for sopping up the juices.

4½ lb (2¼ kg) razor clams
⅓ cup (80 ml) extra-virgin olive oil
2 cloves garlic, crushed
1 tablespoon flat-leaf parsley, minced
1 cup (250 ml) dry white wine
Salt and freshly ground black pepper to taste
6 slices country bread, toasted

To clean clams, scrape them and hold them under cold running water to rinse away sand.

Place the oil in a teracotta pot. Add the garlic cloves and cook over medium heat until garlic is golden. Discard garlic.

Add the minced parsley and the wine. Season to taste with salt and pepper. Cook until wine is reduced by 80 percent. Add the clams, mix thoroughly, and sauté clams over medium-high heat until all of their shells have opened. Place toasted bread in soup plates. Cover with clams and cooking liquid and serve immediately. Serves 6.

"MOLECHE CON IL PIEN"

Stuffed Soft-shelled Crabs (Corte Sconta)

Soft-shelled crabs can only be caught shortly after the crab has molted and are thus considered a delicacy. Tradition dictates that these be served with slices of grilled Polenta (see page 27).

3 eggs
1 tablespoon grated grana cheese
Salt to taste
1½ lb (750 g) live soft-shell crabs
Unbleached all-purpose (plain) flour for dredging
Extra-virgin olive oil for frying

Break the eggs into a large bowl with a tight-fitting lid. Stir in the cheese and add salt to taste. Beat with a fork.

Wash the soft-shelled crabs and submerge them in the beaten egg mixture. Cover the bowl. Turn the crabs occasionally.

After about 2 hours, the soft-shelled crabs will be dead. Clip the tips of their claws and dredge them in the flour, shaking off any excess.

In a large pan, heat olive oil for frying. Submerge the crabs and fry until golden, about 2 minutes. Remove the crabs from the oil with a slotted spoon and place on paper towels to drain. Salt to taste. Arrange the crabs on a serving platter and serve immediately. Serves 6.

SARDONI ALLA GRECA

Greek-style Sardines (Corte Sconta)

Although known as Greek-style, this dish of sardines is as Venetian as they come. For a different take on this dish, try substituting balsamic vinegar for the white wine vinegar given here.

2¼ lb (1 kg) fresh sardines
Bay leaves for lining bottom of dish
1 clove garlic, crushed
¼ teaspoon green peppercorns
Salt to taste
Extra-virgin olive oil for dressing sardines
½ cup (125 ml) white wine vinegar

Clean sardines and debone them, but leave the two halves of each fish attached.

In a skillet, make a bed of bay leaves to cover the bottom. Arrange the sardines on top of the bay leaves. Add the garlic clove and peppercorns and season to taste with salt. Drizzle on a generous amount of olive oil.

Place the skillet over high heat. Pour in the vinegar and cook until sardines are cooked through and the vinegar has evaporated. Remove from heat and allow to cool before serving. Serves 6.

BISATO ANGUILLA SULL'ARA

Salt-baked Eel with Bay Leaves (Fiaschetteria Toscana)

This recipe is a modern rendition of a now extinct practice of baking eel on a hot stone. In times gone by, the glass makers of Murano used a stone, known as an *ara* and set in the entrance of the kiln, to place hot glass on to gradually cool down. The stone withstood very high temperatures and absorbed the heat. The glass workers realized that by placing a whole eel on the hot stone, the extremely high heat would force the fat out of the otherwise fatty eel resulting in a beautifully cooked lean eel. Although it is not possible to approximate such high temperatures at home, this recipe results in deliciously tender and moist eel.

3 1½-lb (750-g) eels
Bay leaves
Rock salt

Preheat oven to 400°F (200°C, gas mark 6).

Make slits about 2 to 2½ in (5 to 6 cm) apart along the backs of the eels. Leave the ends intact. Remove the eel innards through the slits, wash the eels well then immerse in water and vinegar for several hours. Remove and dry thoroughly.

In the bottom of a large casserole, set a wire rack, if you have one, so that the eel fat will drip to the bottom during cooking. Place bay leaves over the wire rack or on the bottom of the casserole if you have no rack. Coat the eels with a small amount of rock salt and place them gently in the casserole. Add additional bay leaves over and around the eels.

Bake in the preheated oven until the eel skin is crispy, about 20 to 25 minutes. Remove from the oven. Remove eels from casserole and transfer to a warm serving dish. Discard bay leaves.

Serve immediately. Serves 6.

SCAMPI CRUDI AL PROSECCO
& CARPACCIO DI PESCE

Scampi with Prosecco & Fish Carpaccio (Al Covo)

SCAMPI WITH PROSECCO

The scampi in this recipe are not cooked, so they must be exceedingly fresh. It's a good idea to refrigerate the serving platter in advance so that it is quite cold.

Fish Carpaccio with bread (left) and Scampi and Prosecco Wine (right).

- **42 very fresh (preferably alive) sushi-grade scampi (see page 31), heads attached and claws firm**
- **10 oz (300 g) valerianella (lamb's lettuce), cleaned, washed, and dried**
- **4 ribs white celery, about 8 oz (260 g), cut in julienne**
- **Salt and freshly ground white pepper to taste**
- **1 teaspoon minced flat-leaf parsley**
- **Juice of $\frac{1}{4}$ lemon**
- **Extra-virgin olive oil for dressing**
- **$\frac{1}{2}$ cup (125 ml) Prosecco di Valdobbiadene sparkling wine (a semi-dry light spumante)**

Peel the scampi, leaving their heads attached. Combine the lettuce and celery and arrange them in a mound in the center of a large, chilled serving platter. Arrange the peeled scampi around the mound of lettuce and celery in a fan-shaped pattern. Season the scampi, lettuce, and celery with a little salt and pepper. Sprinkle on the parsley and drizzle on the lemon juice. Drizzle on a small amount of olive oil. Sprinkle with the wine and serve immediately. Serves 6.

FISH CARPACCIO

Carpaccio usually consists of thinly sliced beef that is often served with olive oil, lemon, and parmesan cheese. In Venice, where fish is abundant, bass receives a similar treatment.

- **1 bass, cleaned, filleted, and cut into thin strips**
- **Mixed salad greens for creating a bed**
- **Salt and freshly ground white pepper to taste**
- **Zest of 1 lemon, cut into julienne**
- **2 scallions (spring onions), minced**
- **Extra-virgin olive oil, preferably from Liguria or Garda, for dressing fish**
- **Bread slices, as needed**

Arrange the salad greens on a cold serving platter. Arrange the bass pieces over the salad. Season to taste with salt and pepper. Sprinkle on lemon zest and minced scallion. Drizzle on olive oil. Arrange bread slices decoratively around the perimeter of the platter. Serves 6.

CANESTRELLI ALLA GRIGLIA
& CAPESANTE IN PADELLA

Broiled Scallops & Sautéed Scallops (Vini da Gigio)

BROILED SCALLOPS

At Vini da Gigio they make this dish using a kind of scallop found in the Venetian lagoon.

2 lb (1 kg) scallops with shells
Salt and freshly ground white pepper to taste
Bread crumbs for topping
Extra-virgin olive oil for drizzling over scallops

Preheat broiler (overhead grill).

Broiled Scallops (left) and Sautéed Scallops (right).

Open the scallops and wash them thoroughly. Leave the scallop meat on half of its shell. Season the scallops to taste with salt and pepper and sprinkle them with a small amount of bread crumbs. Drizzle on a small amount of olive oil.

Arrange the scallops on the broiler pan, shell-side down. Broil until the surface is golden, watching very closely so that they don't burn.

Serve immediately. Serves 6.

SAUTÉED SCALLOPS

This very simple preparation shows off the tenderness of scallop meat.

18 scallops with shells
3 tablespoons extra-virgin olive oil
1 clove garlic, flattened with back of a knife
Salt and freshly ground white pepper to taste
Juice of $\frac{1}{2}$ lemon
1 teaspoon minced flat-leaf parsley

Remove scallop meat from shells. Wash and dry thoroughly. Wash and dry shells and reserve.

In a skillet, heat oil and garlic. Add the scallops, season to taste with salt and pepper, and brown lightly. Remove skillet from heat. Discard garlic. Drizzle on lemon juice and sprinkle on parsley.

Return scallops to their shells and serve immediately. Serves 6.

ALICI MARINATE IN SALSA DI CAPPERI

Marinated Anchovies in Caper Sauce (Corte Sconta)

While you may only be familiar with anchovies in their preserved form—in either oil or salt—fresh anchovies are a true treat. If you can't find fresh anchovies, substitute any small, sweet fish. It is key that the fish be extremely fresh, as it will not be cooked.

Tuna Marinated in Balsamic Vinegar (left, see recipe page 40) and Marinated Anchovies in Caper Sauce (right).

1¼ lb (625 g) fresh anchovies
Juice of 6 lemons, strained
3 cloves garlic, thinly sliced
Salt and freshly ground white pepper to taste
2 oz (60 g) anchovy paste
1–1½ oz (30–45 g) small capers in vinegar, drained and minced
1 sprig wild fennel or dill, leaves minced
3 tablespoons bread crumbs
Juice of 1 large orange, strained
3 tablespoons white wine vinegar

To clean the anchovies, slit them down their bellies and remove their bones, leaving the two halves of each fish attached. Cut off the heads. Rinse and dry thoroughly. In a casserole, arrange the anchovies in a single layer.

In a small bowl, combine the lemon juice and garlic. Season to taste with salt and pepper. Mix well and pour over anchovies. Cover anchovies and marinate for approximately 2 hours, then bring to room temperature before serving.

Just before serving, prepare the caper sauce: Mash the anchovy paste, then mix with the capers, fennel, and bread crumbs. Add the orange juice and vinegar.

Remove the anchovies from their marinade and drain. Discard any garlic stuck to the anchovies. Arrange the anchovies on a serving dish and pour the caper sauce over them. Serve immediately. Serves 6.

RADICCHIO DI TREVISO ALLA GRIGLIA

Grilled Treviso Radicchio (Parco Gambrinus, San Polo di Piave, Treviso)

Grilled radicchio (or red chicory) is a simple yet extraordinary pleasure. When cooked this way, it is sweet, lightly charred, and subtly crispy. Treviso radicchio is the most prized radicchio in the Veneto region and can be identified by its long, pointed leaves that stand away from the central core.

1½ lb (750 g) Treviso radicchio
Extra-virgin olive oil for marinating radicchio
Salt and freshly ground black pepper to taste
2 tablespoons minced Italian parsley

Heat a grill (or wood-burning stove).

Trim the radicchio by cutting away the roots but leaving a small piece at the bottom so that the leaves are still attached to each other. If the tips are wilted, trim them. Cut each bunch in half, cutting vertically and beginning from the root end. Wash the radicchio and dry carefully with a tea towel.

Place enough oil to cover the radicchio in a large dish. Season to taste with salt and pepper. Whisk together, then arrange the radicchio in the dish and let it stand for 5 minutes.

Remove the radicchio from the oil, allowing the excess oil to drip back into the casserole. Reserve the oil. Grill the radicchio until the leaves begin to wilt, about 5 minutes. Drizzle some of the reserved oil over the radicchio, turn it, and cook on the other side.

When the radicchio is cooked, arrange it on a warm serving plate. Sprinkle on the minced parsley and drizzle on additional olive oil if desired. Serve immediately. Serves 6.

INSALATA DI CAPESANTE
CON FUNGHI PORCINI E RUCOLA

Sautéed Scallop, Porcini Mushroom, and Arugula Salad (Ai Mercanti)

This sophisticated salad hails from the Ai Mercanti restaurant in Venice. Although the recipe is not particularly complicated, the results are impressive.

- **1–2 bunches (80–100 g) young arugula, cleaned, washed, and dried**
- **18 scallops in their shells**
- **6 fresh porcini mushrooms (about 25 g each), cleaned and thinly sliced**
- **2–3 tablespoons extra-virgin olive oil**
- **4 tablespoons butter**
- **Salt and freshly ground white pepper to taste**
- **3 tablespoons Worcestershire sauce**

Divide arugula among 6 salad plates.

Shell the scallops and wash them in cold, well-salted water. Dry the scallops. Wash the empty shells well, dry, and set aside. Arrange the empty shells on top of the arugula.

In a saucepan, melt the oil and butter, then add the scallops. When the scallops are cooked, remove them with a slotted spoon and arrange them in the shells. Place the mushrooms in the same saucepan and season to taste with salt and pepper. Cook mushrooms until just wilted. Remove with a slotted spoon and arrange on top of the scallops. Again in the same saucepan, add the Worcestershire sauce to the cooking liquid from the scallops and the mushrooms. Stir and cook until this sauce is fairly dense. Pour the sauce over the mushrooms and serve immediately. Serves 6.

SPAGHETTI NERI ALLE CAPESANTE
& TAGLIOLINI AI CALAMARETTI

Black Spaghetti with Scallops & Tagliolini with Baby Calamari (Corte Sconta)

BLACK SPAGHETTI WITH SCALLOPS

This relatively easy recipe yields quite striking results. Cuttlefish ink spaghetti is black and can be found in specialty stores. It marries particularly well with sauces featuring seafood.

Black Spaghetti with Scallops (left) and Tagliolini with Baby Calamari (right).

4–5 tablespoons extra-virgin olive oil
2 cloves garlic, crushed
18 scallops, cut into julienne
3 medium zucchini (courgettes), cut into julienne
1 cup (250 ml) dry white wine
Salt and freshly ground white pepper to taste
$\frac{1}{3}$ cup (90 ml) fish stock
1 lb (500 g) cuttlefish ink spaghetti
6 cherry tomatoes, halved, seeded, and diced

In a large skillet, heat the olive oil, then add the garlic, scallops, and zucchini and cook briefly until scallops lose their raw appearance. Add the wine and allow to evaporate. Season to taste with salt and pepper. Add the fish stock, stir, and cook an additional 5 minutes. Discard garlic.

Meanwhile, bring a large pot of salted water to a boil. Add the spaghetti. Stir with a long-handled fork and cook until *al dente*. Drain the spaghetti and add them to the skillet with the scallops and the zucchini. Sauté, tossing to combine, for 2 minutes. (Two forks work best for this.) Transfer spaghetti to a warm serving bowl. Top with tomatoes. Serve immediately. Serves 6.

TAGLIOLINI WITH BABY CALAMARI

2 cloves garlic, minced
10 oz (300 g) baby calamari, cleaned
6 tablespoons extra-virgin olive oil
Salt and freshly ground black pepper to taste
$\frac{1}{2}$ cup (125 ml) tomato purée, drained
Tagliolini egg pasta
9 leaves basil, chopped

In a large skillet, cook the garlic and calamari in the oil, stirring often, for 3 minutes. Season to taste with salt and pepper, stir in tomato purée, and cook an additional 5 minutes.

Meanwhile, bring a large pot of lightly salted water to a boil and cook the tagliolini. Separate with a long-handled fork while cooking. When the tagliolini are *al dente*, drain and add to the skillet with the calamari. Cook for 30 seconds, stirring to combine pasta and calamari.

Transfer to a large serving dish. Sprinkle basil over pasta. Serve immediately. Serves 6.

TAGLIERINI ALLA GRANCEOLA

Taglierini with Spider Crab (La Caravella)

Taglierini are thin, fresh egg noodles that add great elegance to this very rich dish. If you want to use dried pasta rather than fresh taglierini, be sure to add on an extra few minutes cooking time. Fresh pasta cooks faster than dried.

4 tablespoons unsalted butter
2 small carrots, peeled and sliced
2 small onions, peeled and sliced
2½ cups (625 ml) dry white wine
1 bouquet garni (comprising 1 bay leaf and
    2 sprigs flat-leaf parsley)
2–3 black peppercorns
Salt to taste
3–4 medium crabs, about 5 lb (2½ kg)
5 tablespoons extra-virgin olive oil
1–2 cloves garlic, crushed
1–2 tablespoons brandy
1 8-oz (240-g) can tomatoes, drained and diced
Taglierini egg pasta
1 tablespoon flat-leaf parsley, finely chopped

To make a court-bouillon, in a large pot melt the butter. Add the carrot and onion slices and cook, but do not allow to brown. Add approximately 2 cups (500 ml) wine, 4 cups (1 liter) cold water, the bouquet garni, and the peppercorns. Season to taste with salt. Bring to a boil, then add the crabs, and cook for 15 minutes. Drain the crabs.

Open the rear of the crabs where the shell is attached and scoop out the meat with a spoon. Dice the crabmeat and set aside.

In a large skillet, heat 3 tablespoons of the olive oil. Add the garlic and brown. Add the diced crabmeat, stir, and cook briefly. Add the brandy and remaining ½ cup (125 ml) wine. Allow the liquid to evaporate completely. Add diced tomatoes and cook, stirring often, for 2 minutes, without allowing tomato pieces to lose their shape. Discard the garlic.

Meanwhile, in a large pot, bring lightly salted water to a boil. Add the taglierini, stir with a long-handled fork, and cook. When the taglierini is *al dente*, drain and add to the skillet with the crabmeat. Cook, stirring constantly, for 2 minutes.

Remove the skillet from the heat. Transfer the taglierini to a hot serving bowl. Drizzle on remaining 2 tablespoons olive oil. Sprinkle on parsley, and serve immediately. Serves 6.

ALGHE DI MARE E MOLLUSCHI

Shellfish and Seaweed (Da Fiore)

The seaweed in this case is spinach pasta that serves as a bed for clams and mussels.

³/₄ lb (375 g) spinach, trimmed, and cleaned
1 lb (500 g) all-pupose (plain) flour, sifted
4 eggs
1¹/₃ cups (330 ml) extra-virgin olive oil
Freshly ground white pepper to taste
2 lb (1 kg) small clams, cleaned
2 lb (1 kg) mussels, scraped and cleaned
3 cloves garlic, minced
1 bay leaf, finely chopped
1 tablespoon celery leaves, finely chopped
1 tablespoon parsley, finely chopped
1 tablespoon basil, finely chopped
¹/₃ cup (80 ml) dry white wine
Salt to taste

Steam spinach in a small amount of water. Drain, rinse, squeeze dry, and blend. On a large wooden cutting board or pasta board, shape the flour into a well. Crack the eggs in the center and beat lightly with a finger. Stir in the spinach. Draw in a small amount of flour from the side of the well and mix with the eggs until you have a paste.

Move the remaining flour from the well on top of the dough and knead to incorporate. If dough is sticky, sprinkle on additional flour. Knead by hand until the dough is smooth and moist, but not sticky or gummy, and spinach is well incorporated, about 8 minutes. Shape the dough into a ball and set aside. Scrape the work surface clean. Flour lightly.

Return dough to floured work surface. Flatten the ball slightly, then roll out the dough, turning it a quarter turn in between each roll. When the dough is ¹/₈ in (¹/₄ cm) thick, complete a final thinning of the pasta by wrapping about one-third of it around the rolling pin and rapidly rolling it back and forth. Cut the sheet of pasta into irregular rhomboid shapes and transfer to a lightly floured tea towel.

In a skillet, heat 2 to 3 tablespoons of olive oil and add a pinch of pepper, the clams, and the mussels. As soon as the clams and mussels open, remove them to a colander set over a large bowl and allow the cooking liquid to collect in the bowl. Remove mussel and clam meat from shells and set aside. Strain liquid that has dripped into bowl and set aside.

In another skillet, heat remaining oil and add garlic, bay leaf, celery leaves, parsley, and basil. Cook, stirring often, for about 10 minutes. Add shellfish cooking liquid, cook for about 2 minutes. Add clams and mussels, season to taste with salt and pepper. Add wine. Cook over low heat, stirring occasionally.

Meanwhile, to cook pasta, bring a large pot of water to a boil. Salt, then add the pasta. Stir with a long-handled fork and cook until *al dente*. Drain and add pasta to the hot pan of shellfish, toss, then transfer to a warm dish. Serve immediately. Serves 4.

BIGOLI IN SALSA

Buckwheat Pasta with Anchovies (Fiaschetteria Toscana)

Bigoli are fresh buckwheat pasta with a wonderful, earthy flavor. They match well with simple sauces like this one.

Bigoli

    1 lb 2 oz (500 g) buckwheat flour
    3 tablespoons butter, softened, cut into pieces
    2 eggs
    Pinch salt
    Milk for moistening dough

Sauce

    $\frac{1}{3}$ cup (80 ml) extra-virgin olive oil
    2 large onions, thinly sliced
    8–10 salt-preserved anchovies, rinsed, deboned, and ground with a little warm water to a paste
    Salt and freshly ground black pepper
    Leaves of 1 sprig parsley, minced

Garnish

    2 salt-preserved anchovies, rinsed, deboned, and filleted

To prepare the **bigoli**, on a wooden cutting board or pasta board, shape the buckwheat flour into a well. Place the butter, eggs, and a pinch of salt in the center of the well. Lightly beat the butter, eggs, and salt with your fingers. Gradually pull in flour from the inside of the well and mix into the egg mixture. Add as much milk as needed to make a thoroughly combined dough that is on the firm side. Form the dough into a ball and allow it to rest for 30 minutes.

Clean off your work surface. Return the dough to the work surface and knead it for a few minutes until malleable. Pass it through a bigoli-making tool, or use a regular pasta machine. As the bigoli are made, spread them out on a lightly floured cloth. Allow the pasta to rest.

In a skillet, heat the oil. Add the onions and sauté very slowly until golden. Add the anchovy paste and stir to combine, season to taste with salt and pepper and cook for a further minute or two.

Meanwhile, bring a large pot of lightly salted water to a boil. Add the bigoli, stir with a long-handled fork, and cook until done. Drain and transfer to the skillet. Warm gently, toss with the anchovy sauce. Transfer to a large warm serving bowl, sprinkle on the parsley and garnish with the reserved anchovy fillets. Serve immediately. Serves 6.

RAVIOLI ALLA ZUCCA CON SALSA DI SCAMPI

Pumpkin Ravioli with Shrimp Sauce (Alle Testiere)

Pasta

- 4 lb (2 kg) pumpkin, peeled, strings and seeds removed, and diced
- 1½ cups (135 g) amaretti, crushed finely
- 1½ cups (135 g) Parmesan cheese, grated
- 1 cup plus 1 tablespoon (135 g) Cremona mustard
- Pinch nutmeg
- Salt and freshly ground white pepper to taste
- Bread crumbs, if necessary
- 1 teaspoon grated lemon zest
- Egg pasta dough

Sauce

- 1 tablespoon unsalted butter
- 1 teaspoon unbleached all-purpose flour
- 35 medium shrimp (prawns), about 1¾ lb (800 g), peeled and cleaned
- 2 cloves garlic, crushed
- 3 tablespoons extra-virgin olive oil
- 2 bay leaves
- 1 tablespoon tomato purée
- 1 cup (250 ml) brandy
- 1 sprig wild fennel or dill, leaves chopped

To prepare the **pasta**, steam or bake the pumpkin until soft then process until smooth. In a large bowl combine the pumpkin purée, crushed amaretti, Parmesan cheese, and mustard. Season with nutmeg, salt, and pepper. Combine thoroughly. This mixture should not be too wet; if it is add a small amount of bread crumbs. Let the pumpkin mixture rest in the refrigerator for at least 12 hours.

When ready to make the ravioli, add lemon zest to the pumpkin mixture. Use a rolling pin to roll out the pasta dough to a uniform thickness then cut into squares. Place a small amount of pumpkin filling on each pasta square. Fold the squares over to form triangles. Press along the edges. Bring the two far corners of the triangles together and press to seal.

To prepare the **sauce**, combine the butter and 1 teaspoon flour until thoroughly incorporated. Form into a ball, wrap in wax paper, and refrigerate until solid. In a large pot, combine the shrimp shells, 4 cups (1 liter) salted water, and the butter and flour mixture that you prepared in advance. Bring to a boil, then lower heat and simmer for 25 minutes. Remove from the heat and strain resulting broth through a fine strainer.

In another pot, brown the garlic cloves in the oil. Add the shrimp, bay leaves, and tomato purée. Season to taste with salt and pepper. Stir to combine and cook until heated through. Add the brandy and allow alcohol to evaporate over high heat. Add the shrimp broth and continue cooking until shrimp are cooked through. Meanwhile, bring a large pot of lightly salted water to a boil. Add the ravioli and cook for 5 minutes. Drain and transfer to a large serving dish. Top with shrimp sauce and serve immediately. Serves 6.

GNOCCHETTI AI CALAMARETTI

Gnocchetti with Baby Calamari (Alle Testiere)

This recipe from Venice's Osteria alle Testiere deliciously combines soft gnocchi with tender calamari. Be sure not to overcook the calamari, as this makes them rubbery.

1½ lb (750 g) starchy potatoes
Unbleached all-purpose (plain) flour for
   gnocchi
3 egg yolks
2 cloves garlic, crushed
3 tablespoons extra-virgin olive oil
10 oz (300 g) baby calamari, cleaned
Pinch cinnamon
Salt and freshly ground white pepper to taste
⅓ cup (80 ml) dry white wine
1 tablespoon flat-leaf parsley, finely chopped

Boil the potatoes in lightly salted water. Drain and, as soon as they are cool enough to handle, peel them. Pass the potatoes through a sieve and let them fall onto a large, lightly floured wooden cutting board. Add a small amount of flour and the egg yolks. With floured hands, knead the potatoes, flour, and yolks, adding additional flour as needed, until you have a smooth, uniform dough. Cut the dough into pieces then, with lightly floured hands, roll them out into ropes about ¾ in (2 cm) in diameter. Cut the ropes into 1-in (2½-cm) pieces and transfer the gnocchi to a well-floured surface. Do not allow the gnocchi to touch each other. Set aside.

To prepare the sauce, in a large pot brown the garlic in the oil. Add the calamari. Season with cinnamon, salt, and pepper. Stir and sauté for 1 minute. Add the wine and 2 tablespoons of water. Cook over medium heat for 5 minutes. Stir and discard garlic.

Meanwhile, bring a large pot of generously salted water to a boil. Add the gnocchi. When the gnocchi float to the surface, remove them with a slotted spoon and add to the pot with the calamari. Add the parsley. Cook over high heat for 1 minute, stirring constantly. Divide the gnocchi among 6 soup plates and serve immediately. Serves 6.

"RISI E BISI"

Rice with Peas (Parco Gambrinus, San Polo di Piave, Treviso)

Risi e Bisi is probably the most famous dish from Venice and the Veneto. The technique used is slightly different than that for a regular risotto, since the rice is added to the broth. It is usually eaten in spring, when peas are at their peak. This dish calls for an honest, dry, young white wine. Try a Piave Tocai Italia.

6 cups (1½ liters) beef broth (approximately)
3 tablespoons butter
2 tablespoons extra-virgin olive oil.
2½ oz (75 g) pancetta, diced
½ onion, minced
1 tablespoon minced flat-leaf parsley
12 oz (375 g) small fresh peas, shelled
Salt to taste
10 oz (300 g) rice
3¾ oz (120 g) grana cheese, grated

Place beef broth in a small pot. Bring to a boil, then turn down and keep at a simmer until needed.

In a large pot, melt the butter with the oil. Add the pancetta, onion, and parsley. Stir over medium heat and allow the onion to become translucent. Add the peas. Salt lightly, and stir with a wooden spoon. When the ingredients are mixed, add approximately ½ cup (125 ml) of the hot broth and cook over medium-high heat.

Add about 4 cups (1 liter) of boiling broth to the pot. Return to a boil and add the rice. Cook, stirring often, until rice is tender. When necessary, add additional boiling broth.

When rice is *al dente*, remove from the heat and finish by adding 2 tablespoons of cheese. Transfer rice to a warm serving dish and serve immediately with remaining grated cheese on the side. Serves 6.

RISOTTO AGLI SCAMPI E RUCOLA

Scampi and Arugula Risotto (Antico Martini)

6 cups (1½ liters) fish fumet or stock
2–3 tablespoons extra-virgin olive oil
10 oz (300 g) scampi (see page 31), shelled
5 oz (150 g) arugula (rocket), trimmed and
  washed
Salt and freshly ground white pepper
¼ cup (50 ml) brandy
2¼ cups (375 g) vialone nano or arborio rice
3 tablespoons butter, softened, cut into pieces
1 tablespoon finely minced parsley

Scampi and Arugula Risotto (left), Artichoke Risotto (center, recipe on page 115), and Risotto with Hops (right, recipe on page 114).

Place fish fumet in a small skillet. Bring to a boil, then turn down and keep at a simmer until needed.

In a large skillet, heat the oil and sauté the scampi and arugula. Sauté for 3 minutes until the arugula is wilted. Season to taste with salt and pepper. Add the brandy and allow it to evaporate almost completely.

Add the rice and sauté, stirring, for 1 minute. Add 2 cups (500 ml) of hot fish fumet and continue to cook, stirring constantly. As the fumet is absorbed, add a little more. Continue to cook this way, adding small amounts of hot fish fumet, until the rice is cooked *al dente*.

Move the skillet off the heat, adjust seasonings to taste, and add the butter. Stir to combine. Transfer directly to a warm serving bowl, sprinkle on the parsley, and serve immediately. Serves 6.

RISOTTO DI GÒ E BEVARASSE

Goby Fish and Clam Risotto (Fiaschetteria Toscana)

Gò, a species of goby, and *bevarasse*, a kind of clam, are found only in the Venetian lagoon—substitute with flatfish and regular clams respectively.

6 tablespoons extra-virgin olive oil
2 onions, minced
2 celery stalks, minced
1 bay leaf
3½ cloves garlic
5 lb (2½ kg) goby fish, cleaned, deboned,
   and filleted (see page 29)
Salt and freshly ground white pepper
3 cups (750 ml) white wine
2¼ lb (1⅛ kg) clams, cleaned
2¾ cups (440 g) vialone nano or arborio rice
1 tablespoon butter
1 tablespoon chopped parsley

In a skillet, heat 2 tablespoons of the oil. Sauté the onion, celery, bay leaf, and 2 cloves garlic until brown. Add the fish. Season with salt and pepper. Cook for 1 minute, then add ½ cup (125 ml) of the wine. Allow wine to evaporate. Add enough water just to cover the fish. Bring to a boil, then lower heat and cook at a gentle simmer for 20 minutes. Discard bay leaf and garlic. Pass fish and cooking liquid through a food mill. Return to skillet and cook, stirring occasionally, until the liquid is well-combined but still has the consistency of broth. Keep warm.

In a large skillet with deep sides, heat 2 tablespoons of the oil. Add 1 minced clove of garlic and cook until golden. Add the clams and 2 cups (500 ml) of the wine. Cover the skillet and raise the heat. Cook clams until they open, removing them as they do and transferring them to a colander set over a bowl. Allow the cooking liquid to collect in the bowl. Remove the clam meat from the shells and reserve. Strain cooking liquid through cheesecloth. Combine strained liquid and clam meat and set aside.

In a large skillet, heat the remaining 2 tablespoons oil. Add the ½ clove minced garlic and cook until golden. Add the rice and cook, stirring, for 1 minute. Add remaining 1 cup (250 ml) wine and allow it to evaporate. Add approximately 1 cup (250 ml) of goby fish broth and continue to cook, stirring constantly. As the broth is absorbed, add a little more broth. Continue to cook this way, adding small amounts of hot broth, until the rice is about halfway cooked. Add the clams and their liquid, and season to taste with salt and pepper. Continue cooking by adding small amounts of goby fish broth until the rice is cooked *al dente*.

Remove skillet from heat and add the butter and the parsley. Stir to combine. Cover the skillet and allow the risotto to rest for 1 minute, then transfer to a serving bowl and serve immediately. Serves 6.

SEPPIE IN NERO &
RISOTTO AL NERO DI SEPPIA

Black Cuttlefish & Black Cuttlefish Risotto (Corte Sconta)

BLACK CUTTLEFISH

The black ink of the cuttlefish gives this dish an almost startling deep color and a pleasantly mild flavor with a hint of brine. Small cuttlefish can be left whole rather than cut into rings. Serve this with grilled slices of polenta, if desired, or use it as a sauce over pasta, or to prepare Black Cuttlefish Risotto.

Black squid ink spaghetti (below left), Black Cuttlefish Risotto (top) and Black Cuttlefish (below right) with grilled polenta.

2½ cups (625 ml) extra-virgin olive oil
1 onion, minced
Salt and freshly ground white pepper
2 lb (1 kg) cuttlefish, cleaned, eyes plucked, sacs removed and reserved, cut into rings
2 cups (500 ml) dry white wine
1 cup (250 ml) tomato purée

Place 2 cups (500 ml) of the oil in a large skillet. Add the minced onion and cook over low heat until golden. Raise the heat to high and add the cuttlefish. Stir and cook for 1 minute. Season to taste with salt and pepper. Open the reserved ink sacs and add ink to taste and to color the mixture to a deep black. Add the wine and allow it to evaporate somewhat. Stir and add the tomato purée. Cook over medium heat, stirring occasionally, for 40 minutes. Add remaining ½ cup (125 ml) olive oil, stir, and cook over medium heat for 5 more minutes. Serve immediately. Serves 6 (see note, right).

BLACK CUTTLEFISH RISOTTO

Cooked Black Cuttlefish may also be used to prepare a delicious and visually stunning risotto.

Half portion Black Cuttlefish (see recipe, left)
2¼ cups (375 g) vialone nano or arborio rice
2 tablespoons extra-virgin olive oil
½ onion, minced
2 cloves garlic, minced
Salt and freshly ground black pepper to taste
6 cups (1½ liters) stock

In a large skillet, heat the oil and sauté the onion and garlic until translucent. Season to taste with salt and pepper. Add the rice and sauté, stirring, for 1 minute. Stir in the cuttlefish mixture then add 2 cups (500 ml) of hot stock and continue to cook, stirring constantly. As the stock is absorbed, add a little more. Continue to cook this way, adding small amounts of stock, until the rice is cooked *al dente*.

Helpful hints: When preparing Black Cuttlefish, note that thick pieces of cuttlefish will take longer to cook. Ensure that you buy cuttlefish with ink sacs (they have often been removed), or look for separate packets of ink which are available from specialty stores. Squid may also be substituted for the cuttlefish.

BRODETTO DI PESCE

Fish Soup (Da Fiore)

Here is Venice's famous fish soup.

$4\frac{1}{2}$ lb ($2\frac{1}{4}$ kg) various fish, such as scorpion fish, catfish, monkfish, skate, dogfish, baby calamari, mullet, and shrimp, cleaned, heads reserved, and cut into slices or fillets

1 onion

1 carrot

1 rib celery

5 cups ($1\frac{1}{4}$ liters) water

1 bouquet garni (comprising 1 sprig flat-leaf parsley, 1 sprig fresh thyme, and 2 bay leaves)

Salt to taste

$\frac{1}{3}$ cup (80 ml) extra-virgin olive oil

$\frac{1}{4}$ cup (30 g) minced onion

2 bay leaves

1 clove garlic

1 tablespoon minced flat-leaf parsley

1 tablespoon minced basil

Freshly ground white pepper to taste

1 cup (250 ml) dry white wine

1 lb (450 g) ripe tomatoes, peeled, seeded, and diced

12 slices country bread, toasted

To make a fish broth, in a large pot combine the reserved fish heads, whole onion, carrot, celery, and the bouquet garni. Add the water and season to taste with salt. Bring to a boil, then lower the heat and simmer for 20 minutes. Strain the resulting broth. You should have about $4\frac{1}{4}$ cups (just over 1 liter) broth. If necessary, supplement it with water. Return the broth to the pot, and bring it back to a simmer.

In a large pot, heat the oil. Add the minced onion, bay leaves, and the garlic and brown. Discard garlic. Add the minced parsley and basil. Stir and immediately add the baby calamari. Season to taste with pepper. Add the wine and allow it to evaporate almost completely. Add the tomato pieces and salt to taste. Discard bay leaves. Add the prepared fish broth and simmer for 5 minutes, stirring occasionally. Return to a boil. Add the dogfish and cook for 5 minutes. Add any remaining fish, except for mullet and the shrimp. Simmer for 10 minutes, stirring occasionally. Add the mullet and shrimp. Return to a boil, then turn down heat and simmer for 5 minutes. Remove from heat.

Divide fish among 6 soup bowls. Pour cooking liquid over fish. Place two pieces of toasted bread in each bowl. Serve immediately. Serves 6.

"SOPA DE PESSE E VERDURE"

Fish and Vegetable Soup (Al Covo)

Extra-virgin olive oil for sautéing, making croutons, and drizzling on finished soup
1 large head garlic, peeled and finely chopped
4 scallions (spring onions), finely chopped
Pinch saffron
4$\frac{1}{4}$ cups (1 liter plus 4 tablespoons) fish stock, made from the heads and bones of the scorpion fish, Saint Peter's fish (John Dory), and bass
1$\frac{1}{2}$ oz (50 g) flat-leaf parsley, finely chopped
$\frac{3}{4}$–1 lb (400–500 g) scorpion fish fillets, about 1$\frac{1}{4}$ in (3 cm) wide
$\frac{3}{4}$–1 lb (400–500 g) Saint Peter's fish (John Dory) fillets, about 1$\frac{1}{4}$ in (3 cm) wide
$\frac{3}{4}$–1 lb (400–500 g) bass fillets, about 1$\frac{1}{4}$ in (3 cm) wide
6 medium shrimp (prawns), slit down the back and the intestinal track removed
2$\frac{1}{2}$ oz (75 g) crab coral, chopped
10 oz (300 g) mussels, well scrubbed with beards removed
4$\frac{3}{4}$ oz (150 g) clams, scrubbed and soaked in well-salted water
Salt and freshly ground white pepper to taste
1 red chile pepper, finely minced
4$\frac{3}{4}$ oz (150 g) cooked cannellini or borlotti beans
3 medium zucchini (courgettes), cleaned and cut in julienne
1 rib celery, cut in julienne
1 medium carrot, cut in julienne
Focaccia or ciabiatta bread, sliced

In a skillet, heat a small amount of olive oil in a skillet and add garlic and scallion. Cook over very low heat, without allowing to brown, for about 10 minutes. Add the saffron and cook over low heat an additional 5 minutes. Add the fish stock and bring to a boil. Lower heat and simmer 20 minutes.

Remove skillet from the heat and allow to rest for about 10 minutes. Strain through a chinois.

In another skillet, over low heat, sauté the parsley in oil. Immediately add a few tablespoons of fish stock. Continue cooking over low heat for 5 minutes. Add the remaining fish stock

In a very large skillet, over high heat and with a little oil, sauté the scorpion fish, Saint Peter's fish, bass, shrimp, crab coral, mussels, and clams, until the shells of the mussels and clams open. This should not take more than 2 minutes.

Season fish to taste with salt and pepper. Add the chile pepper, the beans, the zucchini, the celery, and the carrot to the skillet and cook for 5 minutes.

Pour fish stock and parsley over fish and bring to a boil over low heat.

Meanwhile, brush bread with oil and toast in the oven.

Divide the hot soup among soup bowls. Drizzle on a small amount of olive oil, top with toasted bread, and serve immediately. Serves 6.

VELLUTATA DI PISELLI E BRUSCANDOLI

Pea and Hops Soup (Ai Gondolieri)

This bright green soup makes a lovely luncheon dish.

3½ oz (100 g) pancetta
1 onion
1 sprig rosemary
⅓ cup (80 ml) extra-virgin olive oil plus additional for drizzling on finished soup
½ lb (250 g) peas, shelled
Salt and freshly ground white pepper
6 cups (1½ liters) vegetable broth
5 oz (150 g) hops, washed and finely chopped
Grated grana cheese

Cut half of the pancetta into thin slices and set aside. Mince remaining pancetta together with onion and rosemary leaves.

In a large pot, heat ⅓ cup (80 ml) olive oil. Add the minced pancetta, onion, and rosemary and cook until golden. Add the peas and season to taste with salt and pepper. Cook for one minute, then add the broth. Bring to a boil, then lower heat and simmer for 1 hour, stirring occasionally.

Remove soup from pot and purée in a blender. Return pea purée to the pot, adjust seasonings to taste, and cook over medium heat until thickened slightly to a creamy consistency.

Transfer soup to a warm serving bowl. Sprinkle on hops and reserved pancetta slices. Drizzle on additional olive oil. Serve immediately, Pass the grated cheese on the side. Serves 6.

CREMA DI BORLOTTI CON PORRI E COZZE

Bean Soup with Leeks and Mussels (Quadri)

¾ lb (375 g) dried borlotti beans, soaked overnight, rinsed, and drained
1 onion, chopped
1 carrot, chopped
1 rib celery, chopped
1 lb (500 g) potatoes, peeled and chopped
¼ cup (120 ml) extra-virgin olive oil
2½ oz (75 g) smoked pancetta or high-quality bacon, thinly sliced
5 whole cloves
2 cloves garlic
3 sage leaves
1 sprig fresh rosemary, wrapped with kitchen twine
2 bay leaves
1 scallion (spring onion), minced
Salt to taste
1½ lb (750 g) leeks, cleaned and thinly sliced
3⅓ lb (1½ kg) mussels, well scrubbed with beards removed
2½ oz (75 g) canned peeled tomatoes, drained and diced
1 tablespoon flat-leaf parsley, finely chopped

Place soaked beans in a large pot with the onion, carrot, celery, and potatoes. Add enough cold water to cover and bring to a boil, then turn down to a simmer. Cover the pot with a lid and cook until beans are quite soft, approximately 2 hours, stirring occasionally.

Meanwhile, in a skillet combine 2 tablespoons olive oil, the pancetta, cloves, 1 clove garlic, sage leaves, rosemary, bay leaves, and scallion and sauté. When beans are cooked, add just the oil from this mixture to the beans. Transfer the beans, their cooking liquid, and vegetables that cooked with beans to a blender and purée. Season to taste with salt

Meanwhile, in a skillet, braise the leeks in 1 tablespoon olive oil and approximately ½ cup (125 ml) water. Add salt to taste.

In another skillet, combine 2 tablespoons olive oil and the remaining clove garlic. Add the mussels. Stir with a wooden spoon and sauté until all the shells have opened. Remove the mussels with a slotted spoon and extract their meat. Discard shells.

Transfer the bean purée to a large pot and bring to a boil. Add the braised leeks and the mussels and stir over heat for 1 minute. Transfer to a soup tureen. Sprinkle the diced tomatoes and parsley on top. Drizzle on remaining 3 tablespoons olive oil. Serve immediately. Serves 6.

"PASTA E FASIOI"

Pasta and Beans Soup (Ai Mercanti)

Soupy beans with pasta is one of the most soothing foods in the world and is justly popular. This is the version served at the Ai Mercanti restaurant in Venice. Remember to soak the beans the night before—they should soak for at least 12 hours.

Extra-virgin olive oil for sautéing and drizzling on finished soup
1 sprig fresh rosemary, wrapped with twine
$\frac{1}{2}$ onion, minced
2 cloves garlic, minced
1 rib celery, minced
$1\frac{1}{4}$ lb (625 g) dried beans (preferably from Belluno), soaked overnight, drained, and rinsed
Salt and freshly ground black pepper to taste
$\frac{1}{2}$ lb (450 g) dried pasta, preferably ditalini or linguine

In a terracotta pot, heat the oil and add the rosemary sprig and the onion, garlic, and celery. Sauté briefly, then add the beans. Add cold water to cover by several inches. Season to taste with salt and pepper. Cover the pot. Bring to a boil, lower to a simmer, and then cook, stirring occasionally, until the beans are soft but still slightly *al dente*.

Remove a few spoonfuls of beans with a slotted spoon and reserve. Discard the rosemary sprig. Pass the remaining beans through a food mill. Return the bean purée to the terracotta pot and adjust seasoning. Add the whole beans. Bring to a boil and add the pasta. Stir with a long-handled fork and cook until pasta is *al dente*.

Divide the soup among 6 heated soup bowls. Drizzle a small amount of oil on top and sprinkle on a small amount of additional pepper, if desired. Serve immediately. Serves 8.

"SOPA COADA"

Pigeon Casserole (Parco Gambrinus, San Polo di Piave, Treviso)

This classic Venetian recipe is a casserole made up of layers of bread, pigeon and cheese. Pigeon is usually available , or can be ordered, from specialized butchers.

> 6 cups (1½ liters) beef broth
> 9 tablespoons butter
> 3–4 tablespoons extra-virgin olive oil
> 1 onion, minced
> 2 carrots, minced
> 1 rib celery, minced
> 3 young pigeons, cleaned and plucked, livers reserved
> Salt and freshly ground white pepper to taste
> ⅓ cup (80 ml) dry white wine
> 10 oz (300 g) country bread, cut into medium-sized slices
> 2½ oz (75 g) Parmesan cheese, grated

Preheat oven to 225°F (110°C, gas mark ⅓). Place the broth in a small pot and bring to a boil. Turn down to a simmer and keep at a simmer until needed.

In a large pot, melt about half of the butter and the oil. Add the onion, carrot, and celery and sauté for 2 minutes. Add the pigeons and cook, turning them occasionally, until they are browned on the outside. Season to taste with salt and pepper.

Add the wine and allow it to evaporate completely. Add approximately 2 cups (500 ml) boiling broth and cover the pot. Cook over low heat for 10 minutes. Add the reserved pigeon livers and continue cooking over low heat for another 5 minutes.

Remove livers and drain. Cut livers in half. Remove pigeons and drain. Cut pigeons in half, then debone them, taking care not to break them up into too many small pieces. Pour approximately 4 cups (1 liter) of hot broth into the large pot. Simmer 10 minutes.

Meanwhile, melt the remaining butter in a skillet and toast the bread slices in the butter. Line up some of the bread slices in the bottom of a casserole with very high sides (preferably teracotta). Sprinkle on the Parmesan cheese, then arrange 2 pigeon halves and some livers on top. Continue to layer on bread, cheese, and pigeon and livers in that order until you have used up all the ingredients. The top layer should be a layer of bread with a generous amount of Parmesan cheese on top. Pour the boiling broth mixture over the dish so that all ingredients are wet. Place the casserole in the preheated oven and cook for 1 hour. Add a small amount of boiling broth, occasionally, if needed to keep the dish moist.

Remove the casserole from the oven and serve immediately. Pass additional hot broth on the side. Serves 6.

SEPPIOLINE IN BIANCO CON PISELLI

Small Cuttlefish with Peas (Fiaschetteria Toscana)

The cuttlefish here are almost unadorned, so that their fresh flavor shines through.

Small Cuttlefish Venetian-style on Polenta (left, recipe on page 116) and Small Cuttlefish with Peas (right).

1 tablespoon unsalted butter
1 teaspoon flour
1 large onion, thinly sliced
3 tablespoons extra-virgin olive oil
3 cloves garlic, crushed
3¼ lb (1½ kg) small cuttlefish, skinned, boned, and cleaned
⅓ cup (80 ml) dry white wine
Freshly ground white pepper to taste
Rock salt
2 bay leaves
1 tablespoon flat-leaf parsley, finely chopped
2–3 drops Worcestershire sauce
¾–1 lb (400–500 g) shelled peas
Polenta (see page 27), still warm

Combine the butter and flour until thoroughly incorporated. Form into a ball, wrap in wax paper, and refrigerate until solid.

In a skillet, sauté the onion in the olive oil over low heat until translucent. Add the garlic and allow it to barely turn color. Add the cuttlefish and stir briefly. Add the wine and cook until it has evaporated. Season to taste with pepper and rock salt. Add the bay leaves, parsley, and Worcestershire sauce and continue cooking, stirring occasionally, for 10 minutes. Add the peas and cook another 10 minutes, stirring occasionally. Adjust seasonings.

When the cuttlefish are cooked, add the prepared butter and flour mixture and stir until melted. Discard bay leaves.

Divide the polenta among 6 warm dinner plates. With a spoon, arrange the hot cuttlefish over the polenta. Serve immediately. Serves 6.

"SFOGIE IN SAOR"

Sole in Saor Sauce (Fiaschetteria Toscana)

In the days before refrigeration, the vinegar sauce kept this fish dish from spoiling. It is just as delicious today. Try accompanying this with slices of grilled polenta for a real treat.

6 sole fillets
Freshly ground white pepper to taste
Unbleached all-purpose (plain) flour for
    dredging
½ cup (125 ml) extra-virgin olive oil
2 large onions, thinly sliced
2 bay leaves
Salt to taste
1 oz (30 g) golden raisins
1 oz (30 g) pine nuts
¾ cup (180 ml) white wine vinegar
¾ cup (180 ml) dry white wine

Venetian-style Cod (left, recipe on page 115) and Sole in Saor Sauce (right).

Lightly flatten sole fillets with a mallet (wet the mallet first with cold water to keep it from sticking). Season to taste with pepper and dredge in flour.

In a large skillet, heat about half of the oil over medium heat. Add the fillets in a single layer and cook over medium heat until browned, approximately 6 minutes per side. Remove the fillets with a slotted spatula. Place them in a large non-reactive bowl and season to taste with salt.

In the same skillet where you cooked the fish, add the remaining oil and the onion slices and bay leaves. Season to taste with salt. Stir and cook over medium-high heat until browned. Distribute over sole fillets and sprinkle on raisins and pine nuts.

In the same skillet again, add the vinegar and wine. Reduce by half over high heat. Pour the reduced sauce over the sole fillets. Refrigerate sole until cool and serve cold. Serves 6.

TONNO ALLA VENEZIANA CON POLENTA

Venetian-style Tuna with Polenta (Al Covo)

1½ lb (750 g) white onions, thinly sliced
Extra-virgin olive oil for sautéing
1⅓ cups (330 ml) fish stock, made with fish
  heads, scraps, and bones and then strained
5 bay leaves
3 black peppercorns
1⅓ oz (35 g) raisins, plumped in a small
  amount of white wine, then drained
1 oz (30 g) pine nuts, lightly toasted
Pinch uncooked cornmeal, dissolved in cold
  water, if necessary
2 lb 10 oz (1⅓ kg) very fresh tuna, cut into
  triangular pieces 1–1¼ in (2½–3 cm) thick
Polenta made with 10 oz (300 g) cornmeal,
  fairly soft (see page 27)
Salt to taste

Sauté the onion in a small amount of oil in a skillet. Stir while sautéing over low heat for 5 minutes. Add the fish stock, the bay leaves, and the peppercorns. Cover the skillet and cook over low heat for 25 minutes, stirring occasionally.

Add the raisins and pine nuts. Season to taste with salt. Stir to combine. The aim is to create a mixture of very soft onions. If necessary, to thicken, add the dissolved cornmeal.

In another large skillet, sauté the tuna over high heat in oil. The tuna should be tossed about rapidly so that it cooks on the outside but remains pink on the inside. Add the onion mixture and cook for a few minutes. Arrange the tuna slices on a warm serving dish. Discard bay leaves. Pour onion mixture over tuna. Serve immediately with polenta. Serves 6.

BRANZINO AL VAPORE IN SALSA DI VONGOLE

Steamed Bass with Clam Sauce (Fiaschetteria Toscana)

The steamed fish retains its delicate flavor, accented by a savory clam sauce. Please note that this recipe calls for a steam oven, a specific device made for steam-cooking. You can improvise a steaming system of your own, but you may have to adjust the cooking time.

> 3 cloves garlic, minced
> 4 tablespoons extra-virgin olive oil
> ⅓ cup (80 ml) dry white wine
> 1½ lb (750 g) clams, washed well and soaked in cold salted water for at least 30 minutes
> 1½ lb (750 g) tomatoes, flesh scored with a sharp knife
> 3 basil leaves
> Salt and freshly ground white pepper to taste
> 1 1½-lb (750-g) whole bass, scales removed, washed and cut into 2 fillets with skin on
> 1 tablespoon minced flat-leaf parsley

In a skillet, cook approximately half of the garlic in 2 tablespoons olive oil until golden. Add the wine, then the clams. Sauté until the clams have all opened, then drain in a colander placed over a bowl in order to reserve the cooking liquid. Remove the clams from their shells, reserving the shells. Strain the cooking liquid through a piece of cheesecloth to remove any sand.

Meanwhile, bring a pot of water to the boil and cook the tomatoes for 1 minute. Remove with a slotted spoon, plunge them into cold water, and leave aside to cool. When the tomatoes have cooled, drain them, peel them, cut them in half, seed them, and squeeze out any liquid, then dice.

In a skillet, cook the remaining garlic in 2 tablespoons of olive oil until golden. Add the diced tomato and the basil leaves and season to taste with salt and pepper. Cook the tomatoes for 10 minutes, stirring occasionally, then add the clams and their strained cooking liquid. Stir to combine and adjust seasonings if necessary.

Meanwhile, cut each bass fillet into three equal parts. Place the bass skin-side down in a pot and cook in a steam oven for 10 minutes. Remove the fish from the steam oven, arrange the bass on a serving dish, and cover it with hot tomato and clam sauce. Sprinkle on parsley. Serve immediately. Serves 6.

FILETTI DI SAN PIETRO IN SALSA D'ARANCIA & SCAMPI ALLA BUZARA

St. Peter's Fish in Orange Sauce & Shrimp Buzara-style (Corte Sconta)

ST. PETER'S FISH IN ORANGE SAUCE

Saint Peter's fish (also known as John Dory) has recently become more widely available. This citrus sauce plays it up perfectly.

St. Peter's Fish in Orange Juice (left) and Shrimp Buzara-style (right).

1½ lb (750 g) Saint Peter's fish (John Dory) fillets
Salt to taste
3 tablespoons extra-virgin olive oil
4 thin slices ginger
1 large clove garlic, minced
Pinch dried rosemary leaves, crumbled
1 cup (250 ml) freshly squeezed orange juice
1 tablespoon lemon juice
15 to 20 pink peppercorns
1 tablespoon flat-leaf parsley, finely chopped
6 leaves mint

Arrange the fish fillets in a wide skillet, off the heat, and sprinkle with salt. Drizzle on oil, ginger, garlic, rosemary, orange juice, lemon juice, 1 cup (250 ml) cold water, and the pink peppercorns. Place the skillet over high heat and cover. Cook for 5 minutes. Uncover the skillet and cook over high heat until the cooking liquid has evaporated and a thick sauce has been created.

Arrange the fillets on a serving plate. Pour over the sauce. Sprinkle with parsley and mint leaves. Serve immediately. Serves 4.

SHRIMP BUZARA-STYLE

In this dish from Venice's Trattoria Corte Sconta, shrimp are cooked using the "buzara" method, a method used to cook all kinds of seafood in Venice and the surrounding area. Try this with calamari or mussels, too.

3 cloves garlic, crushed
1¾ lb (800 g) medium shrimp (prawns), cleaned and deveined
3 tablespoons extra-virgin olive oil
1 cup (250 ml) dry white wine
Salt and freshly ground white pepper to taste
¾ cup (180 ml) tomato purée
1 tablespoon bread crumbs
½ golden delicious, or other sweet apple, peeled and grated
1 tablespoon flat-leaf parsley, finely chopped

In a large skillet, cook the garlic and shrimp in the oil. When they turn pink, add the wine. Allow the wine to evaporate. Season to taste with salt and pepper. Add the tomato purée, the bread crumbs, and the grated apple. Stir and cook until the sauce has thickened, approximately 5 minutes.

Discard garlic. Arrange the shrimp on a serving plate. Pour the sauce over the shrimp. Sprinkle on parsley and serve immediately. Serves 4.

PETTO D'ANATRA SPEZIATO
CON PUREA DI MELE E SCALOGNO

Duck Breast with Apple Purée and Shallots (Ai Gondolieri)

Remember to plan ahead when making this delicious recipe, as the duck breasts need to marinate for 24 hours before cooking.

1½ lb (750 g) shallots, diced
1 carrot, diced
1 stalk celery, diced
3 duck breasts (about 3 lb, or 1½ kg)
1 bouquet garni of 1 sprig rosemary and 3 bay leaves
1 cup (250 ml) full-bodied red wine
Salt and freshly ground black pepper
2 apples, peeled and cored
3 tablespoons extra-virgin olive oil
10 tablespoons butter
Pinch dried, crumbled rosemary
Garnish: Seasonal greens sautéed in butter

In a large bowl combine half of the shallots, the carrot, the celery, the duck breasts, and the bouquet garni. Pour in the wine and enough water to cover and set aside in a cool place to marinate for 24 hours.

Preheat oven to 300°F (150°C, gas mark 2).

Remove duck breasts from marinade and place in a baking dish. Discard bouquet garni and about half of the liquid from the marinade. Pour remaining marinade over duck breasts. Season to taste with salt and pepper. Cook in preheated oven for 40 minutes.

Meanwhile, to make the purée, mince the apples together with the remaining shallots. In a skillet, heat 3 tablespoons oil with about half of the butter. Season with dried rosemary, salt, and pepper. Cook for 5 minutes, stirring occasionally, then purée cooked apples.

Melt remaining butter and set aside.

When duck breasts are cooked, remove from oven and cut into ½-in (1-cm) slices. Spoon the apple purée on 6 warm individual plates. Arrange duck slices over purée. Pour melted butter over duck and garnish with cooked greens. Serve immediately. Serves 6.

"MASORIN A LA BURANELLA"

Mallard Burano-style (Vini da Gigio)

1 large mallard, about 4 lb (2 kg), cleaned and plucked, innards removed and reserved (see Stuffing), head removed

Stuffing

4¾ oz (135 g) ground lean beef
3¼ oz (90 g) lard or bacon fat, minced
1 duck liver, minced (see below)
1 duck heart, minced (see below)
Pinch dried rosemary, crumbled
1 rib celery, finely chopped
1 carrot, finely chopped
1/2 onion, finely chopped
1 egg
3¼ oz (90 g) grana cheese, grated
Salt and freshly ground black pepper to taste
Bread crumbs for stuffing

Sauce

3 oz (85 g) unsalted butter
1 oz (30 g) lard
1 rib celery, finely chopped
1 carrot, finely chopped
1 onion, finely chopped
1 clove garlic, crushed
1 bouquet garni (comprising 1 sprig rosemary and 3 bay leaves)
8 black olives, pitted
2 tablespoons capers preserved in salt, rinsed
1 lemon wedge
Salt and freshly ground black pepper to taste
⅔ cup (150 ml) dry white wine
6 cups (1½ liters) beef broth

Wild Duck Burano-style served with Sweet and Sour Onions (for Sweet and Sour Onions recipe, see page 117).

To prepare the **stuffing**, in a large bowl combine the beef and lard. Add the duck liver and heart, the rosemary, celery, carrot, onion, egg, and cheese. Season with salt and pepper. Stir thoroughly and add a small amount of bread crumbs to give the mixture the consistency of stuffing. Combine well then stuff the duck with the mixture. Sew the duck with kitchen thread and tie with kitchen twine.

To prepare the **sauce**, in a large pot, heat the butter, lard, celery, carrot, onion, and garlic. Stir in the bouquet garni, olives, capers, and lemon and cook for 1 minute. Place the duck in the pot and brown on all sides. Season with salt and pepper. Add sufficient wine and broth to completely cover the duck. Bring to a boil, then lower heat and simmer, covered, over medium heat for 1 hour and 15 minutes.

Preheat an oven to 350°F (180°C, gas mark 4). When the duck is ready, remove and drain it, leaving all the liquid in the pot. Place the duck in a baking dish and bake for 10 minutes.

Meanwhile, reduce the cooking liquid in the pot. Discard the lemon wedge and bouquet garni. and pour the reduction into a blender and purée.

Remove duck from oven. Cut away thread and twine. Cut the duck into pieces and the stuffing into slices. Arrange duck and stuffing on a warm serving plate. Pour sauce over duck and stuffing. Serve immediately. Serves 4.

FILETTI DI FARAONA
CON CASTRAURE E TARTUFO NERO

Guinea Fowl Breast with Baby Artichokes and Black Truffle (Ai Gondolieri)

Castraure, or *carciofini*, are baby artichokes and a particular specialty of the Venetian lagoon. The first shoots are pruned early so that only a small number of artichokes are allowed to grow. These are then harvested before they grow to normal size.

½ cup (125 ml) extra-virgin olive oil
2 small bay leaves
3 guinea fowl breasts (abut 2 lb, or 1 kg),
    split, boned, and dredged in flour
6 baby artichokes, cleaned, and quartered
Salt and freshly ground white pepper
⅓ cup (80 ml) dry white wine
⅓ cup (80 ml) beef broth
1 oz (30 g) black Norcia truffle, cleaned and
    thinly sliced

In a large non-stick skillet, heat the oil with the bay leaves. Arrange the guinea fowl breasts in a single layer and brown on both sides. Discard bay leaves and any excess oil. Add the artichokes, season to taste with salt and pepper, and pour in the wine. Bring wine to a boil over high heat. Carefully touch a lit match to the wine and allow the alcohol to burn off.

Meanwhile, place the beef broth in a small pot and bring to a boil. Lower to a simmer and keep at a simmer until needed.

Turn down heat under skillet and cook over low heat for 15 minutes, stirring the artichokes and turning the guinea fowl breasts occasionally. If necessary, add small amounts of hot beef broth to keep birds from sticking. When cooked, add the truffle.

Remove guinea fowl with a slotted spoon and arrange on 6 warm individual dishes. Remove artichokes with a slotted spoon and arrange around the birds.

Deglaze skillet with remaining broth. Pour resulting sauce over guinea fowl and serve immediately. Serves 6.

FARAONA IN SALSA PEVERADA

Guinea Fowl in Peverada Sauce (Vini da Gigio)

Peverada sauce is believed to date as far back as the 16th century. Two other, equally authentic, versions use lemon juice in place of the vinegar and onion in place of the garlic.

6 tablespoons butter
2 guinea fowl (about 2 lb, or 1 kg each),
    plucked, cleaned, livers reserved
Salt and freshly ground black pepper
2 thin slices lard, about 1½ oz (50 g)
3 oz (90 g) chicken livers, cleaned
3 oz (90 g) Venetian soppressa salami
2 salt-preserved anchovies, rinsed, boned,
    and filleted
2 cloves garlic
1 sprig parsley
Zest of ½ lemon
4 tablespoons extra-virgin olive oil
3 tablespoons white wine vinegar

Preheat oven to 350°F (180°C, gas mark 4). Butter a large roasting pan with half of the butter.

Season the guinea fowl inside and out with salt and pepper. Cover the guinea fowl breasts with the lard slices. Truss the fowl, then coat with the remaining butter. Place the birds in the buttered casserole and roast until cooked through, approximately 1 hour, occasionally basting them with their own juices .

To make the sauce, mince together the chicken livers, reserved guinea fowl livers, salami, anchovies, 1 clove garlic, parsley, and lemon zest.

Pour the oil into a medium skillet. Gently cook the remaining whole garlic clove over medium heat until it begins to turn golden, then discard it.

Add the minced ingredients to the skillet and stir with a wooden spoon. Season to taste with salt and pepper. Add vinegar and cook over low heat, stirring almost constantly, until ingredients are cooked through and well-combined, about 10 minutes.

When the guinea fowl are almost cooked through, remove roasting pan from the oven. Untie the birds and remove the lard slices. Return the birds to the oven and cook until golden, about 20 minutes.

Remove guinea fowls from oven. Cut into pieces. Pool sauce on 6 individual serving plates and arrange guinea fowl pieces on top. Serve immediately. Serves 6.

TEGAME DI CONIGLIO E FARAONA
CON BARBA DI FRATE E POLENTA

Rabbit and Guinea Fowl with Garden Cress and Polenta (Ca' Masieri, Trissino)

Barba di frati, literally "monks' beard," is a slightly pungent green called garden cress. It is a close relative of watercress, which is easier to find in some places.

½ large rabbit, skinned, cleaned, deboned, and cut into 6 pieces
½ large guinea fowl, plucked, cleaned, deboned, and cut into 6 pieces
6½ oz (185 g) pancetta, thinly sliced
Salt and freshly ground black pepper to taste
3 sage leaves, minced
¼ teaspoon crumbled dried rosemary
6 tablespoons extra-virgin olive oil
3 tablespoons beef broth, if necessary
1 cup (250 ml) dry white wine
1 bunch garden cress or watercress (about 1½ oz, 45 g), washed, and stems removed
Polenta (see page 27), cooled and cut into slices, then grilled

Preheat oven to 340°F (170°C, gas mark 3½).

Wrap the rabbit and guinea fowl pieces in the pancetta slices. Arrange them in a baking dish. Season to taste with salt and pepper. Sprinkle on the sage and rosemary and drizzle with 3 tablespoons olive oil. Cover the dish with aluminum foil and bake in the preheated oven for 1 hour, turning the pieces occasionally. Should the pan appear too dry, add a small amount of beef broth.

Remove the dish from the oven. Remove the aluminum foil. Pour in wine and return the dish to the oven. Cook until rabbit and pheasant are browned.

Meanwhile, boil the garden cress in lightly salted water. Drain. In a skillet, heat 3 tablespoons of the olive oil and add the cooked greens. Season to taste with salt and pepper. Cook, stirring constantly, for 2 minutes.

Divide the cooked greens among 6 dinner plates. Remove the rabbit and pheasant from the baking dish and place 1 piece of rabbit and 1 piece of guinea fowl on each dish. Strain the cooking liquid from the rabbit and pheasant and use it to moisten the meat. Place polenta slices on each plate.

Serve immediately. Serves 6.

"CASTRADINA"

Lamb Stew (Antico Martini)

Castradina is typically served for the feast of the Madonna della Salute, when Venetians build a bridge of boats across the Grand Canal and then cross that bridge to light candles in the church. This is the version served at the Antico Martini restaurant in Venice.

1 large onion, sliced
3 tablespoons extra-virgin olive oil
$6\frac{1}{2}$ oz (185 g) potatoes, peeled and diced
$3\frac{1}{4}$ oz (90 g) fresh borlotti beans, shelled
$3\frac{1}{4}$ oz (90 g) savoy cabbage, diced
3 ripe tomatoes (about 1 lb, or 450 g), peeled, seeded, and diced
Salt and freshly ground black pepper to taste
10 oz (300 g) castrated lamb, cut into $1\frac{1}{4}$ -in (3-cm) cubes
12 cups (3 liters) beef broth

In a large pot, brown the onion in the oil. Add the potatoes, beans, cabbage, and tomatoes. Season to taste with salt and pepper. Cook for 2 minutes. Add the lamb, stir, then add the broth. Bring to a boil. Lower the heat and cook for $2\frac{1}{2}$ hours, stirring occasionally. Transfer the stew to a serving bowl. Serve warm or at room temperature. Serves 6.

"TRIPPA RISSA CON SALE GROSSO" & "FIGÀ A LA VENEXIANA"

Tripe with Rock Salt & Venetian-style Calf's Liver (Ai Mercanti)

TRIPE WITH ROCK SALT

Tripe, a type of innard, is often found on the tables of Venice.

Tripe with Rock Salt (left) and Venetian-style Calf's Liver (right).

3 bay leaves
Pinch dried and crumbled rosemary
3 black peppercorns
1 rib celery, roughly chopped
1 onion, peeled and halved
1 generous cup dry white wine
2–3 tablespoons extra-virgin olive oil
3¼ lb (1½ kg) tripe, cleaned, soaked in cold
water for 5–10 minutes, and cut into 2-in
(5-cm) strips
Salt and freshly ground black pepper to taste
Rock salt to taste

In a large pot, combine the bay leaves, rosemary, peppercorns, celery, and onion. Lightly season to taste with salt and pepper (remember that you'll be adding rock salt later). Add cold water to cover, wine, and oil. Bring to a boil, then turn down to a simmer and cook for 20 minutes. Add the tripe. If necessary, add additional water to cover the tripe. Cover the pot and cook for at 1½ to 2 hours, stirring occasionally. Remove the tripe with a slotted spoon and divide it among 6 soup plates. Sprinkle on rock salt and moisten with a small amount of the cooking liquid. Serve immediately. Serves 6.

VENETIAN-STYLE CALF'S LIVER

This dish is a real Venetian classic. Traditionally, this recipe calls for equal amounts of onion and liver. Accompany with a dry red wine such as a Piave Raboso.

3 tablespoons butter
3 tablespoons extra-virgin olive oil
1¼ lb (600 g) medium white onions, thinly
sliced
1¼ lb (600 g) calf's liver, cut into ½-in (¼-cm)
slices
Salt and freshly ground black pepper to taste

In a large skillet, melt the butter with the oil. Add the onion slices, stir, then cover and sweat the onion over low for about 30 minutes until completely soft. Stir occasionally to prevent them from sticking. Transfer the onions to a dish.

Reheat the oil to medium high then quickly sauté the liver on both sides until it begins to change color, about 30 seconds.

Transfer the liver to a plate and return the onion to the pan to warm through. Spoon the onion onto a plate and place the liver slices on top. Season to taste with salt and pepper and serve immediately. Serves 4.

CORNETTO ALLE MANDORLE & "BUSOLÀ"

Almond Cakes & Tea Cakes (da Fiore)

ALMOND CAKES

These plain almond cakes are a fitting end to a simple meal, but can also be served in the afternoon with coffee or tea.

>   2 cups (250 g) unbleached all-purpose (plain) flour, sifted
>   6 oz (180 g) unsalted buttered, softened, cut into pieces
>   3$\frac{1}{4}$ oz (90 g) almonds, skinned and ground
> $\frac{1}{3}$ cup (65 g) granulated (caster) sugar
>   Vanilla-flavored powdered sugar as garnish

Preheat oven to 375°F (190°C, gas mark 5).

On a large wooden cutting board or table, shape the flour into a well. In the center place the butter, the ground almonds, and the sugar. Use your fingers to gradually bring more and more flour into the center of the well. Finish by kneading until you have a solid, well-combined dough.

Divide dough into paper-lined or well-greased cup cake tins. Bake in preheated oven for 15 minutes.

Remove from the oven and allow cakes to cool on a wire rack. Sprinkle with sifted icing sugar just before serving. Makes 12 to 16 cakes

TEA CAKES

These cakes can be a dessert or an afternoon snack, and even maks a great breakfast. They go best with some hot tea, but for a fancier presentation, top with some fruit compote.

>   4$\frac{1}{4}$ cups (530 g) unbleached all-purpose (plain) flour, sifted
>   1$\frac{1}{2}$ cups (300 g) granulated (caster) sugar
>   10$\frac{1}{2}$ oz (315 g, or 2$\frac{1}{2}$ sticks) unsalted butter, softened and cut into cubes
>   6 large egg yolks
>   Zest of $\frac{1}{4}$ lemon, grated
>   1 packet powdered vanilla or 1 teaspoon vanilla extract

Preheat oven to 400°F (200°C, gas mark 6).

On a large wooden cutting board or table, shape the flour into a well. In the center place the sugar, butter, egg yolks, lemon zest, and vanilla. Use your fingers to gradually bring more and more flour into the center of the well. Finish by kneading until you have a solid, well-combined dough.

Divide the dough into 16 equal portions and shape them into half-moons or any other shape. Transfer cakes onto a cookie sheet and bake for 18 to 20 minutes.

"PINZA VENEXIANA"

Venetian Cornmeal Cake (da Fiore)

This fruity cornmeal cake has a secret ingredient: grappa, a strong type of brandy.

2 tablespoons unsalted butter, plus additional for buttering pan
1 cup (125 g) unbleached all-purpose (plain) flour, plus additional for flouring pan
4¼ cups (1 liter plus 4 tablespoons) milk
1½ cups (300 g) granulated (caster) sugar
Pinch salt
1½ tablespoons extra-virgin olive oil
½ cup (125 ml) grappa
1¼ cups (200 g) uncooked cornmeal for polenta
3¼ oz (100 g) golden raisins, plumped in warm water and squeezed dry
2 oz (60 g) pine nuts
½ lb (225 g) dried figs, cut into thin strips
1½ oz (45 g) orange, cut into strips
1½ oz (45 g) candied citron, cut into strips
2 eggs, lightly beaten
1 packet powdered vanilla or 1 teaspoon vanilla extract
½ envelope (1 teaspoon) powdered yeast

Preheat oven to 350°F (180°C, gas mark 4). Butter and flour a baking tin. Set aside.

In a pot combine the milk, sugar, salt, 2 tablespoons butter, olive oil, and grappa. Stir to combine and bring to a boil. Add the cornmeal and flour. Stirring constantly, boil for 2 minutes. Add the raisins, pine nuts, figs, orange, and candied citron and lower the heat. Cook over low heat for 30 minutes, stirring constantly with a wooden spoon.

Remove the pot from the heat. Incorporate the eggs, vanilla, and yeast. Stir until ingredients are well-combined.

Transfer to the prepared baking dish and bake in preheated oven for 45 minutes. Serves 6.

FRITOLE

Fritters (Antico Martini)

These simple, warm fritters are a welcome ending to any meal. Like all fried foods, they should be served immediately after they are removed from the cooking oil.

Fritters (left) and Raisin Cookies (right, see recipe page 117).

4 teaspoons fresh yeast, dissolved in a small amount of lukewarm water
2 tablespoons sugar
3 tablespoons melted butter
1 egg
Pinch salt
1¼ cups (160 g) unbleached all-purpose (plain) flour, sifted
Zest of 1 lemon, grated
Zest of 1 orange, grated
½ packet powdered vanilla
1½ oz (45 g) golden raisins, plumped in water and squeezed dry
Oil for frying
Powdered sugar as garnish

In a large bowl, combine yeast, sugar, butter, egg, salt, and flour. Stir to combine. Add enough water to keep the mixture moist, about ⅔ cup (150 ml) in all, stirring between additions until the batter is completely smooth. Stir for an additional 10 minutes once all the flour and water have been added.

Leave the mixture to rise in a draft-free place until almost doubled in size, about 1½ hours.

When the mixture has risen, add the lemon and orange zests, vanilla, and raisins. Stir until completely incorporated, about 2 minutes. Set mixture aside to rise for another 30 minutes.

In a deep pot, heat enough frying oil to submerge the fritters completely. Drop in mixture, about one tablespoon at a time, pushing it off the spoon with another tablespoon to form small balls. Do not overwork the dough. Fry until golden.

Remove fritters with a slotted spoon as they are cooked. Spread them on paper towels to drain briefly. Sprinkle on powdered sugar and transfer to a serving plate. Serve immediately. Makes about 2 dozen fritters.

ADDITIONAL RECIPES

SOPPRESSA SCOTTATA CON RADICCHIO DI CAMPO • SOPPRESSA SALAMI WITH WILD RADICCHIO (CA' MASIERI, TRISSINO, VICENZA)

This rustic appetizer will transport you to the countryside of the Veneto. If you can't find soppressa, use any high-quality salami. See photograph on page 25.

1½ lb (750 g) wild radicchio or other
    radicchio, outer leaves discarded, leaves
    separated, washed, and dried
1 tablespoon extra-virgin olive oil
2¼ oz (65 g) pancetta, minced
1 scallion (spring onion), minced
1 clove garlic, minced
Salt to taste
1¼ lb (625 g) Venetian soppressa salami,
    sliced, but not too thinly

In a large pot of salted water, boil the radicchio until *al dente*. Drain, rinse with cold water, squeeze out as much water as possible, and chop roughly.

Heat the oil in a pot. Add the minced pancetta, scallion, and garlic, and brown. Add the radicchio. Adjust salt to taste. Cook, stirring occasionally, for 2 minutes. Divide the radicchio among 6 small heat-proof plates. Arrange the salami over the radicchio. Run under a broiler until salami is just browned. Serve immediately. Serves 6.

RISOTTO DI BRUSCANDOLI RISOTTO WITH HOPS (ANTICO MARTINI)

Hops are the same plant used to make malt liquor. They abound in the Veneto countryside in early spring. See photograph on page 67.

6 cups (1½ liters) beef broth
1 shallot, minced
2 tablespoons extra-virgin olive oil
10 oz (300 g) hops, washed and finely chopped
⅓ cup (80 ml) dry white wine
2¼ cups (375 g) vialone nano or arborio rice
3 tablespoons butter, softened
3 tablespoons grated Parmesan cheese
1 tablespoon minced flat-leaf parsley
Salt and freshly ground white pepper to taste

Place the beef broth in a small pot and bring to a boil. Lower to a simmer and keep at a simmer until needed.

In a pot, brown the shallot in the oil. Add the hops and season to taste with salt and pepper. Sauté for 2 minutes. Add the wine and allow almost all of the wine to evaporate. Stir in the rice then add approximately 1 cup (250 ml) of hot broth and continue to cook, stirring constantly. As the liquid is absorbed, add a little more broth. Continue to cook this way, adding small amounts of hot broth, until the rice is cooked *al dente*. Move the skillet off the heat and add the butter, the grated cheese, and the parsley. Stir to combine. Transfer directly to a serving bowl and serve immediately. Serves 6.

RISOTTO CON CARCIOFI
ARTICHOKE RISOTTO
(ANTICO MARTINI)

See photograph on page 67.

6 cups (1½ liters) beef broth
2–3 tablespoons extra-virgin olive oil
1 shallot, minced
5–6 artichokes, cleaned and thinly sliced
Salt and freshly ground black pepper
⅓ cup (80 ml) dry white wine
2¼ cups (375 g) vialone nano or arborio rice
Grated grana cheese
1 tablespoon minced parsley
3 tablespoons butter, softened, cut into pieces

Place beef broth in a small pot. Bring to a boil, then turn down and keep at a simmer until needed.
In a large skillet, heat the oil and sauté the shallot until golden. Add the thinly sliced artichokes, season to taste with salt and pepper. Stir to combine and add the wine. Cook until wine has almost completely evaporated. Add the rice and cook, stirring, for 1 minute. Add 2 cups (500 ml) of hot broth and continue to cook, stirring constantly. As the liquid is absorbed, add a little more broth. Continue to cook this way, adding small amounts of hot broth, until the rice is cooked *al dente*.

Move the skillet off the heat and add about 2 tablespoons of grated cheese, the parsley, and the butter. Stir to combine. Transfer to a warm serving bowl and serve immediately. Sprinkle additional grated cheese on the side. Serves 6.

BACCALÀ ALLA VENEZIANA
VENETIAN-STYLE COD

In most places in Italy, baccalà is salt-preserved cod that is soaked in several changes of cold water to rid it of its saltiness, but Venetians use the word baccalà to mean stockfish, or cod that is air-dried but not preserved in salt.
See photograph on page 87.

2 lb (1 kg) dried cod, soaked for 24 hours
    (change soaking water 4 times)
Extra-virgin olive oil
Salt and freshly ground white pepper to taste
¾ oz (25 g) minced flat-leaf parsley
1 clove garlic, minced
Polenta (see page 27), cooled and cut into
    slices, then grilled

Place the soaked dried cod in a large pot. Add cold water to cover. Bring to a boil, skim off any foam that rises to the top, and remove from heat. Cover the pot and let cod soak in warm water for 15 to 20 minutes. Drain the fish. Skin it and remove any bones. Chop the fish into small pieces. In a bowl, stir the fish with a wooden spoon while adding a thin stream of olive oil so that the pieces of fish begin to break down. Continue stirring and adding olive oil until you have a white, creamy, and light mixture. Season to taste with salt and pepper and add the parsley and garlic. Transfer the fish to a serving plate and serve cold, with warm grilled polenta on the side. Serves 6.

MINESTRA DI RISO E LATTE CON CARLETTI • RICE AND MILK SOUP WITH WILD GREENS (CA' MASIERI, TRISSINO, VICENZA)

This comforting soup from the Ristorante Ca' Masieri is terrific on a cold, wintry night. If you can't locate wild greens, use a mix of bitter and sweet leafy greens. It will be just as fortifying. While the method used here is similar to that for risotto, this dish should be much more liquid.

6 cups (1½ liters) milk
3 oz (85 g) unsalted butter, softened and cut into pieces
½ onion (60 g), finely chopped
½ lb (225 g) arborio rice
2½ oz (75 g) wild greens or other greens, washed, dried, and chopped
Grated Grana Pardano or Parmigianno cheese

Place milk in a small pot and heat. Keep at a simmer.

In a large pot, melt 2 tablespoons of butter. Add the onion and cook until golden. Season to taste with salt. Add the rice and cook, stirring, for 1 minute. Add approximately 1 cup (250ml) of hot milk and continue to cook, stirring constantly. As the milk is absorbed, add a little more, maintaining a very liquid consistency. Continue to cook this way, adding small amounts of hot milk, until the rice is cooked.

Add the greens and continue cooking and stirring until greens are wilted, about 1 minute. Taste and adjust salt.

Move the pot off the heat and add the remaining 5 tablespoons butter and the grated cheese. Stir to combine. Cover the skillet and allow the soup to rest for 1 minute.

Divide the soup among 6 soup plates. Serve immediately, passing additional grated Grana Padano cheese on the side. Serves 6.

SMALL CUTTLEFISH VENETIAN-STYLE WITH POLENTA (FIASCHETTERIA TOSCANA)

This is yet another of the delicious dishes served over polenta that Venice has to offer. See photograph on page 95.

⅓ cup (80 ml) extra-virgin olive oil
1 bay leaf
2 cloves garlic, crushed
1 onion, minced
2 lb (1 kg) small cuttlefish, skinned, cleaned, eyes plucked, sacs removed and reserved
Salt and freshly ground white pepper
⅓ cup (80 ml) dry white wine
⅓ cup (80 ml) tomato sauce
1 tablespoon butter
1 tablespoon chopped parsley
Polenta made with ¾ lb (375 g) cornmeal (see page 27)

In a skillet, heat the oil. Add the bay leaf, garlic cloves, and onion and sauté until golden. Discard bay leaf and garlic. Add the cuttlefish. Stir and cook for 1 minute. Season to taste with salt and pepper, then pour in the wine and tomato sauce. Cook over high heat, stirring occasionally.

Dilute the ink from 2 of the reserved sacs with 2 tablespoons lukewarm water. Add to the skillet. Lower heat and cover the skillet. Cook over medium heat, stirring occasionally. If necessary, add small amounts of water to keep cuttlefish from sticking. When the cuttlefish are tender, Stir in butter until melted and sprinkle on parsley.

Distribute polenta among 6 individual plates. Arrange cuttlefish and their sauce over the polenta and serve immediately. Serves 6.

CIPOLLINE IN AGRODOLCE
SWEET AND SOUR ONIONS
(VINI DA GIGIO)

This simple dish from Venice's Vini da Gigio is eaten all over Italy, but sweet and sour preparations are thought to be indigenous to Venice. This can be served as a side dish or appetizer, or even as a salad course. See photograph on page 97.

2 lb (1 kg) small white onions, peeled and washed
Salt and freshly ground white pepper to taste
Dry white wine for sauce
Extra-virgin olive oil for sauce
1 tablespoon golden raisins
⅓ cup (30 g) pine nuts

Preheat oven to 350°F (180°C, gas mark 4).

Arrange the onions in a baking dish. Season to taste with salt and pepper. Mix together equal amounts of wine and olive oil—just enough to moisten the onions—then drizzle over the onions.

Bake for 15 minutes. Turn onions over and bake an additional 15 minutes. Add the raisins and pine nuts. Season to taste with additional salt, if needed. Bake an additional 15 minutes. Serve warm or at room temperature. Serves 6.

ZALETI • RAISIN COOKIES
(ANTICO MARTINI)

Cornmeal and egg yolks give these cookies a beautiful yellow color, which is how they got their name: zaleti means "intensely yellow" in Venetian dialect.

1 cup (125 g) uncooked cornmeal for polenta
1 cup (125 g) unbleached all-purpose (plain) flour
10 tablespoons (4 oz/120 g) unsalted butter, softened, plus additional for greasing pan
½ cup (100 g) granulated (caster) sugar
3 large egg yolks
1 packet powdered vanilla or 1 teaspoon vanilla extract
2 oz (60 g) golden raisins, softened in warm water, then squeezed dry

Preheat oven to 325°F (160°C, gas mark 3).

In a large bowl, stir together the cornmeal and flour. Add the butter and sugar. Beat to combine, then add the egg yolks and vanilla. Knead the ingredients until they are well combined, then work in the raisins.

Turn the dough out onto a marble surface and shape it into logs that are 8 in (20 cm) long and 1¼ in (3 cm) in diameter.

Generously butter a baking pan. Cut the logs of dough into circles about ¾ in (2 cm) thick. Arrange them in the pan and bake in the preheated oven for 20 minutes.

Remove pan from oven. Allow cookies to cool completely in pan. Makes 24 thick cookies.

ACKNOWLEDGMENTS

Sources

Page 45: Plate from Rigattieri

Page 47: Murano glass plate for shrimp and eighteenth-century Murano glass carafes from Al Covo restaurant

Page 49: Cutlery and glasses from Industrie Veneziane

Page 59: Plates from Rigattieri table cloth and napkins from Il Merletto lace school

Page 61: Octagonal red-rimmed glass from Industrie Veneziane

Page 75: Cutlery from Rigattieri

Page 79: Tablecloth and glasses from Venice Home Collection Plate from Rigattieri

Page 85: Table cloths and napkins from Laboritorio Arte & Costume di Monica Daniele

Page 97: Glasses from Venice Home Collection plates and cutlery from Rigattieri table cloth from Il Merletto lace school

Page 99: Plates and cutlery from Rigattieri

Page 101: Cutlery from Rigattieri bowls and glasses from Galleria all'Ascensione srl Vetri Artistici table cloth and napkin from Il Merletto lace school

Page 105: Tablecloth and glasses from Venice Home Collection plates and cutlery from Rigattieri

Page 107: Tablecloth and glasses from Venice Home Collection plates and cutlery from Rigattieri

Page 109: Plate from Rigattieri

Page 113: Salad bowl cutlery and glass from Industrie Veneziane

Page 115: Cutlery silver charger place setting and napkin from Rigattieri

Page 119: Tray from Domus

Page 121: Pewter charger by Rigattieri

Page 125: Glassware from Industrie Veneziane tablecloth and napkin from Il Merletto lace school

Page 127: Glass chocolate bowl and raised cookie bowl (both in background) from Archimede Seguso srl Vetreria Artistica lace tablecloth in background from Il Merletto lace school

Page 129: Tablecloth from Laboritorio Arte & Costume di Monica Daniele plate from Rigattieri octagonal blue-rimmed glass and spoon from Industrie Veneziane

Page 131: Colorful glass bowl from Industrie Veneziane all other plates from Rigattieri

Shops

Archimede Seguso srl Vetreria Artistica San Marco 143, Venezia Tel: (041) 528 9041 Fax: (041) 527 4368

Domus (Articoli Casalinghi Ed Alberghieri) Ruga Rialto 1065, Venezia Tel: (041) 522 3869

Galleria all'Ascensione srl Vetri Artistici San Marco 72/A, Venezia Tel: (041) 522 3129

Il Merletto lace school San Marco 1291 Venezia Tel: (041) 522 9367 Fax: (041) 520 8406

Industrie Veneziane Calle Vallaresso 1320, 30124 Venezia Tel & Fax: (041) 523 0509

Laboritorio Arte & Costume di Monica Daniele is one of a number of small shops that deals in Venetian material tableware and period costumes capturing the spirit of Venetian trading in former times. San Polo 2199 Calle Scaleter Venezia Tel: (041) 524 6242

Rigattieri tra Campo Sant'Angelo e Campo San Stefano, San Marco 3532–36, Venezia Tel: (041) 523 1081 Fax: (041) 522 7623

Venice Home Collection San Marco 95, Venezia Tel & Fax: (041) 520 8406

Restaurants

Antico Martini localita San Marco, via Campo San Fantin 1983, 30124 Venezia Tel: (041) 523 7027 Fax: (041) 528 9857

Ca' Masieri via Masieri 16, 36070 Trissino, Vicenza Tel: (0445) 962100 Fax: (0445) 490455

La Caravella San Marco, via XXII Marzo 2397, 30124 Venezia Tel: (041) 520 8377; Fax: (041) 520 7131 Email: caravella@hotelsaturnia.it

Corte Sconta Calle del Pestrin Castello 3886, 30122 Venezia Tel: (041) 522 7024 Fax: (041) 522 7513

Al Covo Campiello della Pescaria Castello 3968, 30122 Venezia Tel & Fax: (041) 522 3812

Fiaschetteria Toscana San Giovanni Grisostomo Cannaregio 5719, 30131 Venezia Tel: (041) 528 5281 Fax: (041) 528 5521

Da Fiore Calle del Scaleter San Polo 2202/a, 30123 Venezia Tel: (041) 721 308 Fax: (041) 721 343

Ai Gondolieri Dorsoduro 366 San Vio, 30123 Venezia Tel: (041) 528 6396 Fax: (041) 521 0075

Ai Mercanti San Marco 4346/A Calle dei Fuseri, Venezia Tel & Fax: (041) 523 8269

Parco Gambrinus, Localita Gambrinus 22, 31020 San Polo di Piave, Treviso Tel: (0422) 855043 Fax: (0422) 855044 Email: gambrinus@gambrinus.it

Quadri Piazza San Marco 120, 30124 Venezia. Tel: (041) 528 9299; Fax: (041) 520 8041

Alle Testiere Castello del Mondo Novo Castello 5801, 30122 Venezia Tel & Fax: (041) 522 7220

Vini da Gigio Cannaregio San Felice 3628/A, 30125 Venezia Tel: (041) 528 5140 Fax: (041) 522 8597

INDEX

Periplus World Cookbooks
TRAVEL THE WORLD IN YOUR KITCHEN!

Welcome to the world's best-selling international cookery series and the first comprehensive encyclopedia of world cooking. Each volume contains over 70 easy-to-follow recipes gathered in the country of origin. Introductory essays by noted food writers explore the cuisine's cultural roots, and all food photographs are taken on location in the country to ensure absolute authenticity. Truly the ultimate cookbooks for globetrotting gourmets!

"The scope of this small library of books transcends the size of its volumes... They are thoughtful, well-planned, well-edited, and most importantly they strive mightily for authenticity, an effort sadly lacking in so many of today's 'ethnic' cookery books."

"A Gourmet At Large" *Gourmet Magazine*, USA

The Food of Israel
ISBN 962 593 268 2 Hardcover

The Food of Australia
ISBN 962 593 592 4 Hardcover

The Food of Miami
ISBN 962 593 595 9 Hardcover

The Food of New Orleans
ISBN 962 593 594 0 Hardcover

The Food of Sante Fe
ISBN 962 593 596 7 Hardcover

The Food of Texas
ISBN 962 593 534 7 Hardcover